# Service-Learning Companion

# Service-Learning Companion

Dawn Duncan
Joan Kopperud
*Concordia College*

WADSWORTH
CENGAGE Learning™

Australia • Brazil • Japan • Korea • Mexico • Singapore • Spain • United Kingdom • United States

## WADSWORTH
### CENGAGE Learning™

**Service-Learnig Companion**
**Dawn Duncan, Joan Kopperud**

Executive Publisher: Patricia A. Coryell

Executive Editor: Mary Finch

Sponsoring Editor: Shani B. Fisher

Marketing Manager: Edwin Hill

Senior Project Editor: Margaret Park Bridges

Art and Design Manager: Jill Haber

Cover Design Director: Tony Saizon

Senior Photo Editor: Jennifer Meyer Dare

Senior Composition Buyer: Chuck Dutton

New Title Product Manager: Susan Brooks-Peltier

Editorial Assistant: Amanda Nietzel

Marketing Assistant: Erin Timm

Cover Image: © Pierre Tremblay/Masterfile

For product information and technology assistance, contact us at
**Cengage Learning Customer & Sales Support, 1-800-354-9706**

For permission to use material from this text or product, submit all requests online **www.cengage.com/permissions**
Further permissions questions can be emailed to **permissionrequest@cengage.com**

Library of Congress Control Number: 2006937983

ISBN-13: 978-0-618-75898-2

ISBN-10: 0-618-75898-4

**Wadsworth**
20 Channel Center Street
Boston, MA 02210
USA

Cengage Learning is a leading provider of customized learning solutions with office locations around the globe, including Singapore, the United Kingdom, Australia, Mexico, Brazil, and Japan. Locate your local office at **www.cengage.com/global**

Cengage Learning products are represented in Canada by Nelson Education, Ltd.

To learn more about Wadsworth, visit **www.cengage.com/wadsworth**

Purchase any of our products at your local college store or at our preferred online store **www.CengageBrain.com**

Acknowledgment is made to the following sources for permission to reprint selections from copyrighted material: P. 6: Excerpt from Donna Stark, Director, The Learning Patch, reprinted by permission of NTL Institute for Applied Behavioral Science, 300 N. Lee St., Suite 300, Alexandria, VA 22314. 1-800-777-5227. P. 18: "The Experiential Learning Cycle" by David Kolb, reprinted by permission of the author. P. 26: Excerpt from Michelle LeBaron, "Communication Tools for Understanding Cultural Differences." From *Beyond Intractability*. Eds. Guy Burgess and Heidi Burgess. Conflict Research Consortium, University of Colorado, Boulder. Posted: June 2003 <http://www.beyond intractability.org/essay/communication_tools/>. P. 58: Community Model for Conflict Resolution from Rattray, David. "Conflict Resolution Workshop." *First Nations*. CanTeach. Accessed 29 March 2006. <http://www.can teach.ca/elementary/fnations61.html>. P. 65: Excerpt from Working Paper #189, as printed in the journal *Peace and Freedom*, July/August, 1989, "White Privilege: Unpacking the Invisible Knapsack." Used by permission of Dr. Peggy McIntosh, Associate Director, Wellesley College Center for Research on Women. P. 99: Outcomes in a Variety of Courses from Valerius, Laura and Michelle Hamilton, "The Community Classroom: Serving to Learn and Learning to Serve" from *College Student Journal*, Sept. 2001, vol. 35, no. 3, p. 339. Published with the permission of Project Innovation, Inc., P.O. Box 8508, Spring Hill Station, Mobile, AL 36689-8508. P. 125: Poem "I May, I Might, I Must" from *The Poems of Marianne Moore* by Marianne Moore, edited by Grace Schulman, copyright © 2003 by Marianne Craig Moore, Executor of the Estate of Marianne Moore. Used by permission of Viking Penguin, a division of Penguin Group (USA) Inc.

Printed in the United States of America
5 6 7 13 12 11

# Contents

Preface        ix
Acknowledgments        xiii
An Introduction to Service-Learning, *Paul Rogat Loeb*        xv

**Unit I** What Is Service-Learning?
--------------------------------------------------

**1** Defining Service-Learning        3

Service-Learning at a Glance        3
Commitment to Community Partnership        7
Learning and Academic Rigor        11
Intentional, Reflective Thinking        14
Practice of Civic Responsibility        16
The Kolb Experiential Learning Cycle        17
  *Concrete Experience*        *17*
  *Reflective Observation*        *18*
  *Abstract Conceptualization*        *18*
  *Active Experimentation*        *19*
  *The Kolb Cycle in Action*        *19*

**2** Practicing Service-Learning        21

Course-Embedded Service-Learning        22
  *Required or Optional*        *22*
  *Individual or Group*        *23*
  *Short Term or Long Term*        *24*
  *Direct or Indirect Service*        *24*

Other Service-Learning Options        30
  *Campus-wide Initiatives*        *30*
  *Study Abroad*        *31*
  *Alternative Break Programs*        *32*
  *Graduation Requirements*        *33*
  *Beyond Graduation*        *34*

# Unit II Why Do Service-Learning?

**3** Becoming Good Citizens  39

Preparing to Live as Citizens in Community  39
The Value and Virtue of Citizenship  43
Service-Learning in the Aristotelian Tradition  46
Levels of Engaged Citizenship  48
A Personal Case of Engagement  51
Leadership, Conflict Resolution, and Teamwork  55
Avoiding Stereotypes, Acknowledging Privilege,
  and Embracing Diversity  60
  *Race*  61
  *Class*  62
  *Gender*  63
  *Overcoming Stereotypes*  63
  *Privilege*  64
Social Change Wheel  67

**4** Preparing for Your Future  68

Transferable Skills and Intentional Learning  68
Academic and Cognitive Abilities  71
Social and Interpersonal Skills  75
Finding Your Calling  80
Career Understanding, Work Preparedness, and Equipped
  for the Future (EFF) Skills  84

# Unit III How Does Service-Learning Work?

**5** Participating in an Integrated Experience  91

Roles of Service-Learning Participants: Campus Facilitators,
  Community Partners, and Students  91
  *Campus Facilitators*  92
  *Community Partners*  93
  *Student Participants*  94
Identifying Learning Objectives and Outcomes  94
Organizing for Service-Learning Success  101

**6** The CARC Learning Cycle: Contemplation, Action, Reflection, and Commitment    105

Contemplation    107
Action    112
Reflection    115
Commitment    122

Works Cited    126
Index    131

# Preface

Whether you are a first-year or upper-class student, whether you are studying accounting or zoology, this text will help you understand and practice the service-learning method. You have the ability to participate in shaping the direction of your own learning even as you contribute to the well-being of your community. This book provides guidance for you as you practice responsible citizenship in community and directs you to ways in which you can develop leadership skills for your future.

We decided to write this book because of our direct experience with students doing service-learning and our ongoing commitment to the pedagogy. While there are plenty of resources for teachers and administrators, few textbooks speak directly to you, the students, and are applicable in any discipline. As one reviewer indicates: "This [book] is the first effective resource I have read intended to engage the students in [service-learning]—it encourages students to become a part of the process, rather than a subject for the process."

The chapters are presented in a logical way that will help you build from a basic understanding of what service-learning is to the complex practice of the method. **Unit One, "What Is Service-Learning?"** defines the pedagogical method and explains various ways in which it might be practiced on a college campus and in the community. **Unit Two, "Why Do Service-Learning?"** provides the theoretical foundation of good citizenship, gives specific guidance for developing team and leadership skills, and helps prepare you for meaningful work in the world now and in the future. **Unit Three, "How Does Service-Learning Work?"** moves you into your direct experience of service-learning, helps you recognize what roles various people will play during this experience, and provides a framework called the CARC (Contemplation, Action, Reflection, Commitment) Learning Cycle that will help you engage powerfully and productively in the process. Use the CARC Learning Cycle to complete and reflect on service-learning projects. This cycle draws attention to the distinctively different types of thinking that occur during the stages of service-learning. As you read the text and apply the ideas to your own service-learning experience, we encourage you to keep a journal so that you can chart your own growth and understanding.

Each chapter has the following features:

- **Learning objectives** at the beginning of each chapter clearly outline the chapter's concepts and purpose.

- **Focus exercises** in each chapter include several steps to help you apply, reflect, or act on the relevant content.
- **Tip boxes** include effective strategies for participating in service-learning projects.
- **Online Study Center** icons appear throughout the text to alert you to material corresponding to the book's website. Visit **college.hmco.com/pic/duncan1e** for additional ways to *Improve Your Grade* and *Prepare for Class*.

In addition to the material contained in *Service-Learning Companion,* there are supplementary resources available for instructors:

- An **Online Teaching Center** offers instructors the authors' Instructor's Resource Manual. Visit **college.hmco.com/pic/duncan1e** to explore the Online Teaching Center.
- The **Instructor's Resource Manual** will help you use *Service-Learning Companion* in your course. The IRM includes a variety of helpful tools: learning objectives, sample syllabi, and forms and handouts. If you are just starting out, use this guide to help you begin integrating service-learning into your class.
- **Noel-Levitz College Student Inventory (CSI)** is the leading retention and enrollment management consultant for higher education in the United States. Its main product is the Retention Management System (RMS)—an early-alert, early intervention program that identifies students with tendencies that contribute to dropping out of school. At the heart of the RMS is the College Student Inventory (CSI) assessment surveys that evaluate students on several scales that predict the likelihood that a student will stay in school. This system can be packaged with any Houghton Mifflin textbook at a discounted price, and is available online and in print. Please contact your Houghton Mifflin sales representative for more details.
- The **Myers-Briggs Type Indicator® (MBTI®) Instrument,**[1] the most widely used personality inventory in history—is also available for packaging with *Service-Learning Companion.* The standard Form M self-scorable instrument contains ninety-three items that determine preferences on four scales: Extraversion-Introversion, Sensing-Intuition, Thinking-Feeling, and Judging-Perceiving. Talk to your sales representative about completing the qualification form for administering the MBTI on your campus. Contact your Houghton Mifflin sales representative for more details.
- **Houghton Mifflin College Survival Consulting Services**. Houghton Mifflin College Survival consultants are higher education instructors, administrators, or student service professionals who have experience

---

[1] MBTI and Myers-Briggs Type Indicator are registered trademarks of Consulting Psychologists Press, Inc.

teaching the Student Success course. Teachers and administrators of Houghton Mifflin client schools can call 1-800-528-8323 or email collegesurvival@hmco.com to contact specially trained College Survival consultants for assistance with any stage of program development. Use your consultant to help establish, maintain, and grow Student Success courses.

• **Workshops/National Conferences**. Houghton Mifflin College Survival sponsors workshops and conferences throughout the year (check the website for current dates and locations). Our one-day workshops are designed for faculty development and feature hands-on, group interaction. Conferences provide two to three days of informative, interactive sessions covering a range of topics presented by authors, Student Success instructors, and College Survival consultants. Information about upcoming workshops and conferences can be found at **http://college.hmco.com/collegesurvival/resources/instructors/ conferences.**

• **Year-Round On-Site Teacher Training and Curriculum Consultation**. One- and two-day regional or on-campus trainings can be arranged for Student Success course instructors, counselors, and administrators of Houghton Mifflin client schools. These training sessions present effective pedagogical strategies that can be applied to all disciplines and that have been proven effective in a variety of Student Success course curricula.

• **Annual Scholarship Essay Contest**. Each year Houghton Mifflin College Survival offers three $1,000 scholarships to outstanding first-year students who provide thoughtful, compelling answers, in writing, to the question "How do you define success?" Find out more about this opportunity by visiting the Houghton Mifflin College Survival website.

# Acknowledgments

In the process of developing this text, we have had the assistance and encouragement of many fine people. We take this opportunity to acknowledge those individuals to whom we wish to express our deepest gratitude. First, we express appreciation to Shani Fisher, Sponsoring Editor, whose initial belief in us sent us on a journey that moved us from teacher/practitioners to authors and theorists in the field; Andrew Sylvester, for assisting with initial editing; Amanda Nietzel, Editorial Assistant, for attending to details; and the Houghton Mifflin Student Success and Education team for helping bring this project to fruition. Chelle Lyons Hanson, Director of Student Leadership and Service at Concordia-Moorhead, first introduced us to the service-learning movement, helped us shape our practice and pedagogy, encouraged us to present and publish, and acted as a willing responder in the course of preparing this text. We are grateful to our colleagues at Concordia College, especially those in the English Department and the Principia Program, for their ongoing support and encouragement. We would like to thank all of our students, from whom we have learned so much, but especially Angie Pfeiffer and Matt Benson, our student research assistants who provided an important student audience and assisted with a multitude of tasks.

We would also like to acknowledge the reviewers who have made valuable contributions to this book:

Melody M. Actouka, *Northern Marianas College*, CNMI
Bahati Banks, *Morehouse School of Medicine*, GA
Michael Bark, *Wisconsin Indianhead Technical College*
Rick Bialac, *Georgia College and State University*
JoAnn Campbell, *Minnesota Campus Compact*
Pauline Chandler, *Antioch New England Graduate School*, NH
Donna Chapa Crow, *University of North Carolina at Wilmington*
Kristen Christman, *University of North Carolina at Greensboro*
Kevin Corcoran, *University of Cincinnati and Northern Kentucky University*
Lina Dee Dostilio, *Duquesne University*, PA
Janet Eyler, Peabody College, *Vanderbilt University*, TN
Ryan Fewins, *Saginaw Valley State University*, MI
Mary Beth Ginter, *Pima Community College*, AZ
Aileen Hales, *Boise State University*, ID
Ann Hernandez, *University of St. Francis*, IL
Julie Johnson, *Concordia University*, IL

Tony Johnson, *Florida State University*
Claire King, *Indiana University*
Kevin LaNave, *St. Cloud Technical College*, MN
Chelle Lyons Hanson, *Concordia College*, MN
Tania D. Mitchell, *California State University*, *Monterey Bay*
Donald Mowry, *University of Wisconsin-Eau Claire*
Luciano H. Ramos, *Florida Campus Compact*
Tanya Renner, *Kapi`olani Community College*, HI
Amy Rupiper Taggart, *North Dakota State University*
Brian Shmaefsky, *Kingwood College*, TX
Kara Stack, *North Dakota University*
Larry Thomas Meade, *Points of Light Foundation* and *National Volunteer Center National Network*, DC
Barbara Wallace, *Northern Kentucky University*
Mara Wasburn, *Purdue University*, IN
Kate Williams, *Eastern Kentucky University*
Penelope Wong, *California State University*
Laurie E. Worrall, *Depaul University*, IL
Connie Renee Zornes-Padovani, *Sinclair Community College*, OH

Finally, we want to express our love and gratitude to our husbands and families for their patience, devotion, and steadfast belief in us.

*Dawn Duncan*
*Joan Kopperud*

# An Introduction to Service-Learning

*Paul Rogat Loeb*

We hear a lot about the retreat of students from public life. Annual surveys suggest that students care less each year about the environment, racial understanding, community-action programs, or even discussing political issues. Your generation has been repeatedly accused of apathy—simply not caring. Yet as I travel to speak, visit classes, and lead workshops at campuses throughout the country, I see less indifference and more learned helplessness—the feeling that you can't change the world, so why try?

Wherever I go, small groups of students do tackle the critical issues of our times: environmental threats, illiteracy, growing gaps between the rich and the poor. But many feel too overwhelmed. They do important work volunteering one on one because that's tangible and concrete. But when asked to imagine themselves taking on the deeper roots of issues they care about, they come up blank. Our culture hasn't given then the models to take action.

Our cultural myths suggest people are either socially active or not: A few saints or crazies storm out of the womb with protest signs in their hands, but the rest of us are normal and leave the messy business of changing society to others. The two paths never cross. But people change their values, perspectives, and commitments when given the right opportunities—and grow in powerful ways.

A student at Fairfield University in Connecticut is a good example. Tim is a wealthy doctor's son. "We gave the blacks a lot," Tim said, when I interviewed him as a first-year student. "Is it my fault if my parents or I make the bucks so they can't?" He wondered whether racial inequality was "maybe biological."

"I want the things I have now," Tim explained, "a nice house, a nice car, a nice boat. I want to make enough to buy a place of my own, where . . . if someone's bothering me, I can say 'Buddy, buzz off, this is mine. This is what I've paid for.'"

Then Tim began to learn and to think. He was a pre-med student when a young professor introduced environmental issues in his organic chemistry class. At first Tim resisted, he said, then he started listening. Soon he joined a campus environmental group and went into environmental remediation as a career. Now he cringes at his earlier attitude. He says that had his teacher not had the courage to raise difficult public issues, he never would have changed.

To foster engagement, we need teachers willing to challenge us and listen to us. We need strong examples to overcome what psychologist Robert Jay Lifton calls the "broken connection" between our values and actions, between the world we inherit and the one we pass on. We need to understand the barriers we face, like our society's pervasive cynicism and growing economic pressures.

It's easy to wait before getting involved. Many of us feel a lack of confidence based on trying to live up to a "perfect standard" for ourselves. Before we take a public stand on an issue, we think we need to know every fact, figure, and statistic, and be eloquent enough to debate Henry Kissinger on *Nightline*. We feel we have to be as eloquent as Martin Luther King Jr. and as saintly as Gandhi. We also feel we need perfect confidence in our passion for the issue, our motives for taking it on, and the certainty that it's the most urgent cause imaginable. But those who actually make a difference are always ordinary human beings with ordinary hesitations and flaws. They act despite their fears and help change the world in small or not so small ways.

To overcome the barriers to involvement, we need examples of people, present or past, who take action despite their doubts and uncertainties, and keep on despite apparent failures. This book provides those examples as well as practical lessons on how to get involved and what it can mean to our lives.

Rosa Parks is one of the few activists whose name most of us know. Many people think that Parks came out of nowhere to change history in an instant when she refused to move to the back of a Montgomery, Alabama, bus. Yet before refusing to give up her seat on the bus, Parks had spent twelve years in a leadership role with the local NAACP chapter. The summer before, she'd attended a ten-day training session at Tennessee's labor and civil rights organizing school, the Highlander Center, where she'd met an older generation of civil rights activists and discussed the recent U.S. Supreme Court decision banning "separate but equal" schools.

In other words, Parks didn't come out of nowhere. She didn't singlehandedly give birth to the civil rights movement. She didn't act alone, or on a whim. Instead, she was part of an existing struggle for change at a time when success was far from certain. That in no way diminishes the power and historical importance of her refusal to give up her seat. But it reminds us that this tremendously consequential act might never have taken place without the tireless efforts she and others had made earlier on. It reminds us that her initial step of getting involved was just as courageous and critical as the fabled moment when she refused to move to the back of the bus. It refutes the myth that anyone who takes a committed public stand—or at least an effective one—must be a larger-than-life figure, someone with more time, energy, courage, vision, eloquence, and knowledge than any normal person could ever possess.

We need to know this history, to have a sense of what it takes to act and persist for a difficult cause. As a student from West Virginia told me recently, "They teach the conclusions: 'Lincoln freed the slaves. Women got the vote. Some unions were organized.' We never learn how change actually occurred." We need to learn how it occurs, how people come together with a common voice, and what our own role could be. We need to find ways to act.

This book helps us do this. It shows us examples of how to act and persist, how to link seemingly modest community efforts with larger global questions. I hope it helps teach you how to take a stand. For if we aren't going to step up to try and shape a common future, who will?

*Paul Rogat Loeb*

Paul Rogat Loeb is the author of *Soul of a Citizen: Living with Conviction in a Cynical Time* and *The Impossible Will Take a Little While*: *A Citizen's Guide to Hope in a Time of Fear*. See **www.paulloeb.org** for more on his work. Copyright Paul Rogat Loeb.

# What Is
# Service-Learning?

# Defining Service-Learning

## Service-Learning at a Glance

*Each week Kendra volunteers at First Harvest Food Pantry, where she stocks shelves with donated food items. Kendra is providing an important* **service** *to her community.*

*Eric is taking a course titled This American Life as one of his general education requirements. Through lectures, readings, and class discussions, students learn about social issues, such as hunger, that confront Americans today. A guest speaker explains how First Harvest Food Pantry responds to hunger needs in the local community. Eric is* **learning** *about contemporary American social problems.*

*Lisa is majoring in nutrition at an area college. For one*

### LEARNING OBJECTIVES

After studying this chapter and doing the exercises, you should be able to

- Define *service-learning, volunteerism, community-based*
- Identify the four traits that characterize service-learning
- Distinguish between *service-learning* and *volunteerism, community service,* and *internship/cooperative education*
- Explain how communities are formed, and identify communities to which you belong
- Locate information about your community partner
- Identify goals and objectives for your service-learning experience
- Practice intentional reflective thinking
- Understand the concept of active citizenship and its connection to service-learning
- Identify and describe the stages of the Kolb Experiential Learning Cycle

*of her courses, Lisa and her classmates serve at First Harvest Food Pantry every week throughout the semester. As they fill food orders, they attend to such concerns as nutritional balance, medical conditions, and cultural considerations as part of their learning goals. Lisa also keeps a reflective journal to explore connections between what she is learning about nutrition in class and what she is seeing, doing, and learning at the food pantry. She draws from her service experience during class discussions about nutrition, hunger in America, and the roles and responsibilities of citizens. Lisa seeks to apply new theories and understandings about the complex issue of hunger*

3

*as she continues her service at First Harvest. Lisa is participating in* **service-learning***.*

Reflect on these scenarios. What do they have in common, and how do they differ? What do your answers tell you about service-learning? To help you comprehend the differences and more clearly understand what you are about to undertake as a participant in service-learning, study the following definition: *Service-learning is a teaching and learning method that upholds a commitment to appreciating the assets of and serving the needs of a community partner while enhancing student learning and academic rigor through the practice of intentional reflective thinking and responsible civic action.* Analyze the definition so that you can see how each key idea in the definition corresponds to Lisa's work. Discuss your ideas with a partner or a small group. You have just done a focus exercise. The purpose of a focus exercise is to help you engage with the text and apply the material to your learning experience.

As a participant in service-learning, you are part of a firsthand learning experience that creates intentional reciprocal partnerships between you and your community. Those who incorporate service-learning to address learning goals adhere to the philosophy that students and community-service partners offer one another valuable assets and resources. When community and classroom are directly and thoughtfully connected, each is enhanced.

More and more college students are participating in off-campus firsthand experiences as part of their higher education. All across college campuses, community-based learning is occurring in various forms. Consider these diverse examples. Every spring the men's basketball team volunteers to help host Special Olympics in the community. A print journalism major works at the local newspaper for her senior year internship. The university chapter of a fraternity performs community service by holding the campus blood donation drive every fall. An elementary education major earns course credit for the cooperative learning experience of organizing and leading an after-school reading program. Are all these community-based experiences service-learning? Not necessarily. Terminology related to community-based learning—such as *volunteerism, community service, internship,* and *cooperative education*—are often used interchangeably with *service-learning,* but the other terms describe experiences different from service-learning.

## Four Traits That Characterize Service-Learning

1. Commitment to community partnership
2. Learning and academic rigor
3. Intentional reflective thinking
4. Practice of civic responsibility

Many students have volunteered with organizations such as 4-H, Big Brother Big Sister, local community boards, and youth groups. Most often, *volunteerism refers to people who freely give their time to provide some kind of service or assistance without expecting anything in return.* When you volunteer, the primary emphasis is on the service provided to others, and the intended beneficiaries are the service recipients. For example, once a year Adam volunteers with the Special Olympics event in his town. He registers contestants and participates as a finish-line encourager. Though Adam may feel good about his volunteer work, this feeling is a consequence, not a specific learning objective.

For some people, the term *community service* refers to court-ordered volunteer work, for example, as part of a court-ordered sentence for a drunk driving conviction. Others have a different understanding of the term, which suggests *opportunities in the broader community for individuals to work to meet real community needs.* For example, clearing litter from roadside ditches through the Adopt-a-Highway program is community service. As with volunteer work, the service provider is not the main beneficiary.

Students may be beneficiaries of community-based learning experiences in programs such as *internships* and *cooperative education.* Participating in an internship or cooperative experience means receiving *supervised practical training at a work site.* Most internship and co-op opportunities emphasize the application of a particular skill set related to a major field of study. For example, if you are an accounting major, you might engage in an internship or co-op experience at a national accounting firm to learn more about how large accounting firms operate. Most often, the purpose of your internship or co-op experience is career preparation or the opportunity to explore a particular career possibility. Internships and cooperative experiences are varied, and participants may work in paid or unpaid positions and serve in either for-profit or nonprofit organizations. In some instances, an internship or co-op learning position might be considered a service-learning experience if it meets the four traits that characterize service-learning (see sidebar), but in most cases, the emphasis is still on career preparation.

While service-learning incorporates acts of volunteerism and community service and may even be undertaken during an internship or co-op experience, it is different because it emphasizes benefits to both those served and the service provider. Quality service-learning experiences reflect a balanced reciprocal relationship between you and the community partner based on mutual respect for the assets and resources of each.

Another important distinction is that service is always directly connected to specific learning objectives. These objectives are formulated for a particular course, major, core college requirement, or cocurricular activity. They are a chief consideration by both the learner and the community partner, which ensures equal responsibility and a balance of benefits through the service-learning partnership. This concentration on learning objectives also separates service-learning from other types of community-based learning.

You may have entered into this experience thinking that you are engaged in service-learning only because of perceived community needs. However, it is important to recognize and appreciate that community-service partners also offer you such benefits as valuable hands-on experiences, practical knowledge, and insight into yourself, others, and the world around you. For instance, Elise, a first-year college student, was helping provide appropriate early childhood playtime activities at a local government-supported child-care center as she studied how values are imparted to children in various cultural contexts. Her service-learning experience helped her overcome her shyness and even led to self-understanding and a career decision. She came to recognize that she is better at working one-on-one with specific tasks than working with groups, causing her to change her major from elementary education to occupational therapy with an emphasis on children. Also through her service-learning experience, Elise gained a deeper understanding of the importance of subsidized nonprofit daycare for low-income parents. Just as Elise benefited from the service-learning experience, so did the center that she served. As Donna Stark, Director of the Learning Patch, writes,

> The staff and children at our childcare center have found that the service-learning that the students do has been such a benefit for everyone involved. We, the staff, receive the extra help and hands that we need with the children, and the children and students benefit from the positive connections that they make with each other. This is a wonderful way for students to get out into the community to give of their time and receive so much in return.

Elise and her community partner provide a paradigm of the benefits when service and learning are effectively joined: Individuals grow and communities improve because of the assets each offers the other.

The service-learning method offers you the chance to practice critical thinking and problem solving in complex real-life situations. As you read this text,

you will see how service-learning students implement problem solving and critical thinking. As you participate in your own service-learning experience, you will find yourself adapting to complex situations and developing your own critical thinking and problem-solving skills. When service-learning is effectively implemented, you not only gain new knowledge and understanding, but you also develop as an individual and a citizen. Continue to keep the four traits of service-learning—commitment to community partnership, learning and academic rigor, intentional reflective thinking, and practice of civic responsibility—in mind.

# Commitment to Community Partnership

Advocates of service-learning believe that individuals are integrally connected to broader communities and that all citizens have a responsibility to serve, support, and work toward positive change and social justice in those communities. That is why the first essential trait of service-learning calls for meaningful service in a community-based setting. Most often *community-based* means that *the learning partnership occurs at the local level, likely within the city or town in proximity to the classroom or cocurricular setting.* However, based on a broader understanding of community, even the college campus can become the service-learning community partner. For example, a college environmental studies class or an environmental club can engage in meaningful service within its own college community by researching and documenting campus recycling efforts and then presenting scientific findings to the college administration to effect positive changes in policy. A flexible definition of *community* is possible as long as the learning partnership meets the other three criteria that characterize service-learning—learning and academic rigor, reflective thinking, and civic responsibility.

To understand the ways in which communities may be flexible, consider that communities are most often constructed with regard to commonality, meaning that members of a community share certain aspects of life. They may be based on geography, such as neighborhoods; culture, such as nationality or ethnicity; principles, such as political or religious beliefs; interests, such as hobbies or social organizations; or physical characteristics, such as age or gender. Communities offer people the opportunity to connect with each other and to enrich their lives through those connections.

Consider Sergio and the many communities with which he identifies. He lives in the International House on campus, which has created a geographical neighborhood for him. As a Brazilian from São Paulo, he identifies ethnically with other Brazilians and South Americans and also with other Portuguese speakers. His religious community is large because he is a practicing Catholic, though he appreciates a smaller sense of community with his local parish. Sergio is active in the intramural soccer program and enjoys both playing and watching soccer with his teammates, establishing a community based on both interest and peer group. As you can see, Sergio experiences community at many levels, from the worldwide Catholic community to his small group of soccer

teammates. He feels a sense of connection in all these communities because of what he shares with others in each group.

Though communities often share some commonality, individuals within a community may differ widely. That variety within community also enriches even as it sometimes challenges. In the International House, Sergio lives among students who come from different parts of the world, practice different religions, speak different native languages, and prefer foods that are foreign to Sergio's experience. For instance, his roommate, Sanjiv, comes from Nepal, practices Buddhism, and cooks vegetarian meals. Even on his soccer team, Sergio must learn to appreciate community members with varying techniques and ability levels. When Sergio embraces not only the similarities but also the differences of community members, his own life is enriched. He now has a wider set of friends who have taught him much, from new recipes to new ways of coordinating team play. Individual differences in community provide essential and enriching variety.

As you think about community, try to identify the wide variety of communities to which you are connected, not just those whose members are similar to you. For example, you are part of your college community because you have many similarities with others who also have chosen to attend your institution, but you are also part of the broader community in which your college resides. In the future you will add more communities to your life, and not all of them will be based on similarities. Your service-learning experience may place you among neighbors and friends or among people with whom you are less familiar, but all are part of your community. Before you begin

## FOCUS EXERCISE

### Exploring Communities

#### A. Identifying Personal Communities

Consider your geographic home, your cultural identity, the principles on which you stand, your interests and hobbies, your age, and your gender. Make a list of the many communities to which you belong. Circle one of the communities to which you feel strongly affiliated. What are the similarities you share with members of this community? What are notable differences among the community members? How does the community enrich your life?

#### B. Appreciating the Wider Community

Doing any research that is necessary, list aspects of the community in which your college resides. Who lives in this area? What is their cultural background? Is the geographic area best described as rural, town, or metropolitan? What are the demographics of this area—average age, income, education, employment opportunities, and so on? What do you have in common with the wider community? Consider carefully those aspects that are diverse from your personal experience. What might these different aspects of community offer as you learn and grow?

service, it is helpful to understand your connectedness to communities and how community is formed. Take time to complete the focus exercise that helps you explore communities.

Once you recognize all that community has to offer you, you are more likely to want to serve on behalf of community. However, your desire is not enough to establish a good service relationship. It is essential for your service to be meaningful and valuable to the community, to provide something the community desires. To create a successful service-learning experience, you must respect the community-service partner for its assets—for the strengths and benefits it brings to the wider community. Service-learning is partnership-based, and you should consider not only your own goals and objectives but also how you can help support the community partner's goals and objectives. Look through the eyes of your partners and listen to what they say about their mission, what they see as their vision of themselves. Then you will be ready to determine how best to meet a specified need that originates with the community and is part of its vision.

The community partner determines and expresses particular needs; service providers do not suggest what the partner needs. For example, students serving at a community theater expected to be needed to build sets and sew costumes. However, the theater's mission goes beyond theatrical entertainment to a responsibility for enriching the entire community through educational and service opportunities. To fulfill that mission, the nonprofit theater most needed a successful annual fundraiser, and this large undertaking required the help of the students. Because the students were part of a liberal arts seminar focused on the theme of community, the learning objective dealt with recognizing and meeting community needs. Consequently, the

**F**OCUS EXERCISE

### Considering Community Partner Issues

Look at the Tip Box, Information You Need to Learn about Your Service Site, to help you complete this exercise. If your community partner is already selected, what do you think the partnership has to offer you? What need do you think you will primarily be meeting through your service? Learn more about your community partner by searching the Internet, attending a site orientation, obtaining materials from the community partner, and/or interviewing a staff member at your service site to determine the mission, assets, and needs of the agency. What new information did you learn? How will this affect your understanding of your service and your appreciation for what the experience may bring to you?

*Answer 6 out of 12*

**!** **INFORMATION YOU NEED TO LEARN ABOUT YOUR SERVICE SITE**

Use the following questions to help you discover what you need to know about your service site. Use your research and interviewing skills to complete the answers to as many questions as possible.

1. What is the community partner's mission? Does it have a mission statement? If so, make note of the statement. Ask if informational brochures about the organization are available.

2. What is the history or background of the organization?

3. What services does the community partner provide for the wider community? What need(s) do these service(s) fill? Look for supporting statistics from informational brochures and/or a site orientation.

4. How does the local need compare with the national need?

5. What major issues, obstacles, or challenges do individuals served by the community partner face on a day-to-day basis?

6. Where does the money to fund this organization come from? Does the organization receive adequate funding at the present time? What does the funding for the future look like? Besides financial support, what other ways does the broader community support this organization?

7. How many paid staff members are employed at the agency? What role does the staff seem to play on a regular basis for those served by the organization?

8. How many unpaid workers serve at the agency? What are different ways unpaid workers serve the organization?

9. How will you spend your time assisting your community partner?

10. What are the special issues you need to be aware of in your role at the service site?

11. Is there additional information you would like to note?

12. What additional questions do you have about your community partner, its clients, and the issue area?

activity was negotiated to fit both the partner's need and the learning objectives, and the students spent their time stuffing envelopes with letters requesting support. The students learned a valuable lesson about the difficulty of obtaining funds to support the arts. Through thoughtful communication, careful planning, and effective negotiation of needs, a successful partnership between learners and community can be established so both benefit. A mutually respectful reciprocal relationship is a central tenet of successful service-learning.

# Learning and Academic Rigor

The second trait that characterizes service-learning is academic rigor. The name *service-learning* makes it apparent that learning is an essential component of this community-based educational philosophy. In fact, when facilitators—teachers or other directors—consider incorporating the service-learning approach to teaching and learning, they begin by identifying desired learning outcomes. For example, instructors ask, "What do I want students to know, to do, and to be like by the end of this course? What kind of community-based service experience will provide opportunities for students to accomplish the course objectives and will also address genuine community needs?" By answering such questions in collaboration with community partners, educators begin to shape powerful and effective academic service-learning experiences. You may want to think about the personal goals and objectives you would like to achieve from service-learning.

If service-learning is to be recognized as a legitimate method of teaching and learning, the service learning experience must provide a rigorous academic challenge. This is why most service-learning is connected to a formal learning experience such as a class setting, where academic credit is earned for the learning that takes place. Instructors who choose service-learning as a teaching method are aware of the limitations of traditional methods. As early as the 1960s, the National Training Laboratories studied the most effective teaching methods and developed what is now called the Learning Pyramid.

## FOCUS EXERCISE

### Identifying Learning Objectives

Look at your syllabus and go over your notes from the introduction (if any) to service-learning or the overall course. Identify learning objectives. How do they relate to the decision to use the service-learning method? How might this pedagogy enhance your learning? Contemplate what you would like to learn from service-learning. What do you want to know, do, and be like by the end of the experience? Write at least two personal goals for the service-learning experience. How might the process of serving your community partner and reflecting on the experience help you meet these goals?

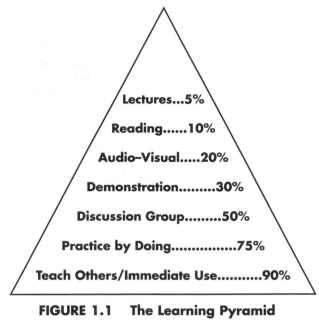

**FIGURE 1.1    The Learning Pyramid**
Source: National Training Laboratories, Bethel, ME.

The pyramid stipulates the average retention rate of information based on various teaching methods. Look at Figure 1.1, and note that the most effective methods, those that ensure the highest retention rates, depend on active experience.

All the teaching methods included in the Learning Pyramid are important and may contribute to your learning. It is likely that your instructor will sometimes give lectures. You are involved in reading by virtue of engaging with this and other texts. Your instructor may also include demonstrations or employ audio or visual technology. However, these methods account for successful retention rates of 30 percent or less; while each provides valuable learning experiences, more active strategies are also necessary.

Your professor has recognized the power of active learning and has integrated the service experience. With your peers and community partners, you will engage in discussion that increases recall and solidifies the learning experience. Most significantly, your retention rate will improve dramatically when you practice by doing at your community site, putting the theories and skills you are learning to immediate use. Because service-learning is an active pedagogy, it will assist you in achieving your current objectives and will make the learning transferable and long term.

Service-learning provides rigorous learning experiences that deepen, enrich, and expand your knowledge and understanding in multiple ways beyond the course for which it is assigned. It forces you to think critically and to apply your learning in a public situation. Teachers in classroom settings require and encourage critical thinking and active learning, but the public sphere adds a new dimension and new possibilities for applied learning. Community partners become coeducators, sometimes reinforcing learning and other times exposing tensions or inaccuracies and bringing problems with theory to light. Broader, deeper learning occurs through service-learning because the method connects theory from the classroom with practical life in the community.

For example, as part of their course learning, students in a social work class visited new American families to help identify, understand, and assist with socialization needs, such as how to use public transportation and where and how to access free recreational facilities. Issues that students had not considered, such as gender roles and social modesty, created tensions about the immigrants' uses of public transportation and recreational facilities. The students had to negotiate these tensions to appropriately assist the new immigrants in becoming socialized without losing their ethnic identities. In this case, course content was enriched by the service experience, and the social work students gained firsthand knowledge about the life experiences, gifts, hopes, challenges, and needs of a particular population in the community. Students stretched their intellectual capacities by using transferable skills such as problem solving as well as social and presentation skills. They worked to synthesize practical information with their course content to better help their community partners and to take their learning to a new level. As this example indicates, service-learning experience blends intellectual, moral, and civic opportunities to create a rigorous academic experience.

Higher-level critical thinking skills such as analyzing, reasoning, decision making, problem solving, investigating, and synthesizing are an essential part of the learning that occurs in service-learning. The service experiences are designed to enhance and extend the learning and the cognitive retention of important academic concepts. The service experiences, course assignments, and follow-up activities are directly connected to course or cocurricular goals and objectives. Evaluation methods are also directly connected to the commitment to academic rigor. Courses that include or are based on a service-learning component may measure student learning with traditional evaluation methods such as exams or essay assignments or nontraditional evaluation methods such as photographic essays or classroom debate, further positioning service-learning as a valuable form of teaching and learning. The community-service partner may be consulted during the evaluation process to ensure that the relationship has been reciprocal. Chapter 5 discusses learning outcomes and evaluation procedures at greater length.

# Intentional Reflective Thinking

A third trait that characterizes service-learning is the expectation of intentional reflective thinking. In fact, the expectation of ongoing meaningful reflection to help you prepare for and process the experience is part of what separates service-learning from volunteering or other forms of experiential learning such as internships. Chapter 6 addresses reflective thinking at length, but it is important to understand that you will use this skill throughout your service-learning activities.

Reflection is an essential component of service-learning that helps you draw meaning from your service experience by connecting it to specific learning content. Intentional reflection challenges you to explore perspectives, stories, questions, and feelings that you bring to the service experience, as well as the kinds of insights, stereotypes, and reactions that emerge from those experiences, and then to connect to or even challenge other learning content. Reflective thinking takes many forms, often involving writing, speaking, or another form of expression that helps you make sense of your service experience in a thoughtful, reflective manner.

For example, Whitney F., a student whose service-learning took place in a daycare facility, wrote the following:

> I feel that my patience skills are improving every week I serve at The Learning Patch. Having patience is so crucial around the kids. They need time and space to learn from their own mistakes. I've also found that it is very important to explain *why* something is wrong or right. The kids don't understand if they are just told not to do something, because they may think what they are doing is just fine . . . until they are told why their actions aren't right. It's just as important to praise the kids and let them know that they are special. My service at The Learning Patch is teaching me a wealth of information about the institution of daycare, kids, and my own personal character.

Whitney was reflecting on both what she learned about the subject at hand—the role of daycare in constructing character values—and what she learned about herself—her need for patience. A next step might call for her to analyze her own values in light of her experience and evaluate whether they are on or off target. Additionally, she could observe a particularly patient daycare employee, attempt to model that behavior, and discuss her growth in this area with a coworker. Following this series of activities, Whitney would once again reflect on what she learned and how she learned it. Ultimately, reflection offers you the opportunity to explore the complexity of service in community from multiple perspectives.

## FOCUS EXERCISE

### Practicing Reflective Thinking from Multiple Perspectives

Take a moment to reflect on a powerful learning experience in your life that you shared with at least two other people. What happened? What did you learn from the experience? Now place yourself in the position of the other people who shared the experience and imagine how they would describe it. Having reflected on the experience and the differing perspectives, either through writing or drawing, describe or illustrate what you learned from trying to view the experience from multiple perspectives.

Reflection throughout the service-learning experience helps you prepare more effectively for, and then draw new knowledge and understanding from, the experience. Reflection may be incorporated in your service-learning experience in many ways, but the emphasis always must remain on the learning journey and how the experience challenges and connects to the rest of your course or cocurricular learning content. Reflection that merely tells what happened during the service experience falls short of authentic, meaningful service-learning reflection. By contrast, effective reflection digs deeper into the meaning of the experience, striving for new insights that can be applied to the practice of service-learning as you continue your work.

# Practice of Civic Responsibility

The fourth trait characterizing service-learning is the emphasis on practicing civic responsibility. Rapidly changing demographics; global tragedies such as hurricanes, tsunamis, and terrorist attacks and escalating world tensions challenge all citizens to consider their roles and responsibilities.

3. The United States has long promoted the principle that citizens have a civic responsibility to contribute to the good of the community. Because a democracy is government of, by, and for the people, it depends on the goodwill and action of the people to sustain it. The U.S. educational system is historically grounded in the principles of democracy. To maintain a healthy democracy, education must prepare citizens to act and live responsibly, which includes forming considered public judgments, breaking down social barriers that hinder social justice, practicing conflict resolution, and developing ethical leadership. Benjamin R. Barber, an internationally renowned political theorist who is a leader of Democracy Collaborative and a distinguished professor at the University of Maryland, argues that

> The remedy is not better leaders but better citizens; and we can become better citizens only if we reinvigorate the tradition of strong democracy that focuses on citizenship and civic competence. This calls for participation as well as accountability; for civic duty as well as individual rights. It demands that we add the constructive use of public judgment and power to the already well established protection of private rights and strong interests. (169)

Service-learning helps you exercise civic competence as you participate in the community. This experience enacts the kind of citizenship that Barber argues is necessary to a democracy.

## FOCUS EXERCISE

### Examining the Power of the Citizen to Act

**Theory:** Harry Boyte, codirector of the Center for Democracy and Citizenship at the Humphrey Institute of the University of Minnesota, encourages us to reverse the axiom to think globally and act locally, urging that "The phrase should be, instead, something like 'think locally and learn to act with impact on the larger world'" (175). What does his statement mean to you? What are its implications for your service-learning participation with your community-service partner?

**Application:** List three political issues that are currently of concern at the local level. Are any of these issues beyond the ability of ordinary citizens? Should they be left to professional politicians? Explain your stance. About which of the issues do you feel competent to reach some kind of public judgment—that is, an informed decision—that would affect your behavior in the wider community? What effect might your public judgment and corresponding action have on the larger world? In a small group, discuss the issues and possible actions you identified. Can any of these issues be addressed during your service-learning experience?

In a democracy, all citizens have an obligation to work for, among other things, justice, peace, and equality. Curricula, texts, discussions, and experiences should challenge you to think critically about a wide range of public issues related to community and responsible citizenship—in short, about your civic obligations. However, reading about and discussing public policies and social issues is not enough. To truly live up to your responsibilities as a citizen, you should work to achieve and sustain social justice in your community. To act responsibly, to serve, and to lead, you need to develop social and civic competencies. Firsthand experiences based in a rigorous learning setting can help you develop the necessary skills for full lifelong participation in a democratic society. A college education enhanced by service-learning experiences directly connects you to your community and others so that you can explore your role in the world. Chapter 3 discusses the role of civic responsibility and its connection to service-learning at greater length.

# The Kolb Experiential Learning Cycle

Educators have long been concerned with civic responsibility and making sure that they can actively apply the theories they espouse. Service-learning, which was born out of the marriage of theory and action, is firmly in the category of experiential education. Based on the twentieth-century work of philosopher John Dewey, psychologists Kurt Lewin and Jean Piaget, and others, experiential proponents value firsthand experiences outside of the traditional classroom as the foundation of learning.

Inspired by the work of Lewin, educational psychologist David A. Kolb identified a four-part learning process based on firsthand experience in which knowledge is created. Although Kolb's landmark work has led to many adaptations, including the CARC cycle to which you will be introduced in Chapter 6, the basic principles identified in Figure 1.2 show how your service-learning experience moves through important stages of learning.

Note that learning cannot be reduced to simple or distinctly separate sequential steps. The cycle does not intend to imply that each step is completed in isolation and leads to the next. Rather, think about how a wheel is continually in movement. Your learning will be similarly fluid and continuous.

The four central points of the Kolb learning cycle are concrete experience, reflective observation, abstract conceptualization, and active experimentation. Kolb's model suggests that the learner may enter the cycle at any stage of the process and that stages often overlap; for effective learning to occur, the learner must move through all four phases of the process. Learning should focus on small, incremental steps, providing opportunities for the cycle to repeat many times, rather than passing through each of the phases once.

## Concrete Experience

This stage of the learning cycle is *characterized by doing*; that is, you carry out *action in a community-based setting*. At this stage of learning, you are immersed in performing some kind of task or participating in some kind of

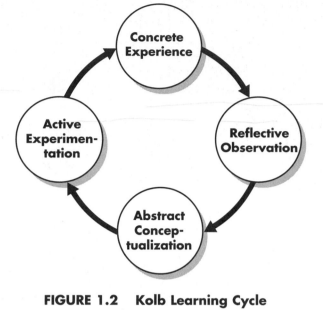

**FIGURE 1.2    Kolb Learning Cycle**
Source: Atherton. Adapted by Kolb.

experience firsthand. During the concrete experience stage, learners "must be able to involve themselves fully, openly, and without bias in new experiences" (Kolb, "Learning Styles" 236).

## Reflective Observation

In the Kolb cycle, concrete experience provides the basis for reflection. However, it should be noted that reflection is crucial throughout the entire service-learning process. Reflective observation is *characterized by re-viewing—that is, re-seeing or mentally revisiting—what has occurred or what you have experienced during the concrete stage.* Through writing, discussion, or some other means of expression, you explore the concrete experience and your perceptions. At this stage of the cycle, learners also must "observe and reflect on these experiences from many perspectives" (Kolb, "Learning Styles" 236).

## Abstract Conceptualization

This stage is *characterized by interpreting your concrete experience and reflective observation in light of other learning, theories, or related concepts.* You now use your firsthand experience and reflection *to build new ideas, theories, or understandings.* Here is your opportunity to affirm or challenge previous assumptions to develop a better theory, which you will test in the next stage of active experimentation. During abstract conceptualization, you strive to understand the relationship among aspects of the course content

and your experiences to explain, modify, or frame the events and to connect to or integrate with a broader perspective. Kolb reminds learners that they "must be able to create concepts that integrate their observations into logically sound theories" ("Learning Styles" 236).

## Active Experimentation

Active experimentation occurs when *learners translate new understandings into action or plan what action will occur next.* At this stage, newly developed understandings and theories guide new experiences. Kolb believes that learners must "use these theories to make decisions and solve problems" ("Learning Styles" 236).

## The Kolb Cycle in Action

To look at the Kolb cycle in an actual learning situation, we apply it to the experience of Sophie, a first-year student enrolled in a composition course that incorporates the service-learning experience as the basis for research and writing assignments. Because of her interest in psychology and adolescent development of middle school girls, Sophie has chosen to serve for two hours each week in the YWCA Empowerment for Girls after-school program at a nearby middle school. Sophie mentors seventh and eighth grade girls. Discussions and activities focus on topics such as successful leadership and interpersonal skills for young women.

Each week Sophie immerses herself in the **concrete experience** by planning, organizing, and leading activities and discussions that will help develop

## FOCUS EXERCISE

**Tracing a Learning Experience Using the Kolb Experiential Learning Cycle**
Choose a recent significant learning experience. Using the Kolb learning cycle, trace your learning from concrete experience through active experimentation. Did you move through all four phases, or was some part of the cycle missing from your experience? How does considering the cycle help deepen your understanding of the learning process?

leadership skills in the middle school participants. Sophie strives to remain open to all dimensions of her actions and experiences to gain a deeper understanding of adolescent psychology. She then records **reflective observations** in her field journal, a required writing assignment in which she explores her observations, perceptions, and thoughts about the service experience in order to connect to course content and reach new understandings and insights.

Sophie next moves into **abstract conceptualization** to deepen her learning experience. For class, Sophie recently read *Queen Bees and Wannabes: Helping Your Daughter Survive Cliques, Gossip, Boyfriends, and Other Realities of Adolescence* by Rosalind Wiseman, an assigned text based on her choice of service sites. By participating in class discussions and writing an assigned critical analysis, Sophie interprets events from her service experience in light of Wiseman's theories and assertions about adolescent girls. Sophie finds herself modifying her understanding of adolescent development as she challenges Wiseman's theory and synthesizes her concrete experience, reflection, and abstract conceptualization. For Sophie, new questions and theories about middle school girls' behavior continually emerge.

Each week, Sophie is eager to return to the YWCA Empowerment for Girls program to check out her new understandings of adolescent girls, which have emerged from action, critical thinking, course readings, writing, and discussion. During the **active experimentation** phase, Sophie uses what she has observed and learned to effectively interact with and mentor program participants. Throughout the semester, Sophie repeatedly moves through the four phases of the Kolb learning cycle in order to create new layers of knowledge about herself, her service site, and the world around her.

By now, you should have a better understanding of service-learning and of how it creates a balanced and reciprocal relationship with community partners. You have learned initial theory that will soon be put to the test in your service-learning experience. The next step in your theoretical learning, Chapter 2, will help you more fully understand the kind of service-learning experience you are entering.

# Practicing
# Service-Learning

**2**

A growing number of colleges and universities across the country are turning to service-learning in its myriad forms—required or optional, individual or group, short term or long term, direct service or indirect service. In fact, a nationwide coalition of more than a thousand campuses known as Campus Compact is "committed to educating students for responsible citizenship in ways that both deepen their learning and improve the quality of community life" ("Our Vision"). The organization's executive director, Elizabeth Hollander, underscores the importance of the service-learning movement: "Campuses across the country are taking unprecedented steps to be active contributors to American democracy. These statistics show that community service is vital to the college experience, and that colleges are increasingly fulfilling their public purposes, to serve communities and educate citizens" (qtd. in Campus Compact, "Record Numbers").

**LEARNING OBJECTIVES**

After studying this chapter and doing the exercises, you should be able to

- Recognize and describe the various types of service-learning experiences, and explain how they differ from one another

- Identify the differences between direct service and indirect service as well as the challenges and benefits of each

- Explain the difference between high-context and low-context communicators and the strategies each must employ for effective communication

- List at least three important communication tips to remember as you practice service-learning

- Articulate how your specific service-learning experience is constructed and fits into the various kinds described in this chapter

- Recognize the service-learning options available on your campus

- Recognize available postgraduation service-learning options

Not only are colleges stepping up to fulfill their civic and educational responsibilities, but students are also seeking opportunities to serve. A recent article in *The Chronicle of Higher Education* reports that "Two out of three college freshmen say it is essential or very important to help others who are in difficulty, the highest percentage in a quarter century. A record number, '83 percent,' say

21

they volunteered at least occasionally during their senior year of high school" (Hoover). More and more students are coming to higher education with some kind of volunteer experience, and many expect continuing opportunities to blend meaningful service to the community with their academic learning.

Chances are good that your service-learning experiences will be enriching. Your institution probably offers a variety of options. Service-learning is frequently embedded within a course, but this is not always the case. Many colleges incorporate service-learning in freshman orientation, or you may participate through a campus organization. Although no two service-learning experiences are identical, quality service-learning experiences always reflect an important balance: Your service experience will inform the learning objectives, and the learning objectives will inform your service experience. No matter how the experience is framed, the learning and outcomes should benefit both you and the community.

# Course-Embedded Service-Learning

## Required or Optional

Often service-learning is a significant component of courses. Such courses may be found in virtually every discipline and department. Required service-learning embedded within a course is frequently the primary method of student learning, substituting for or complementing more familiar methods of teaching and learning, such as lectures and textbook reading. Think of the service-learning experiences as chapters in a living textbook that can yield rich information, new experiences, and powerful learning opportunities.

At one institution, for example, students in a Spanish class study intercultural communication, bilingual and immersion education, and immigration. The students use their Spanish while assisting, interpreting, translating, and teaching in various community organizations. Required service-learning like this provides an opportunity for a powerful connection between academic content and course objectives, since the broader community is the basis for discussions and assignments.

When service-learning is a course requirement, the professor assesses the learning that occurs. Most often, a portion of the course grade is based on some kind of product, project, presentation, or other demonstration of learning derived from the combined service and learning experiences, not on the service alone. In some instances, students earn participation points for working at their service sites, and the participation points are included in the total points earned for the course. The community partner may provide input for assessment. If you are engaged in service-learning for a course, look at your course syllabus and materials to ascertain what bearing your service-learning experience will have on your overall grade and how your learning will be assessed.

Not all instructors require service-learning participation; sometimes service-learning is one of several learning options in the course. For example, in a political science course offered at one college, students choose from three options for their final projects: to write a traditional academic research paper based on

scholarly resources from the library; to conduct interviews and produce a qualitative paper based on careful analysis of interview data; or to participate in a service-learning experience. In this last option, students serve a required number of hours at a service site with which the professor has established a community partnership and in which community needs and student learning are balanced. For the political science course, students who choose the service-learning option keep reflective journals throughout the service experience and also produce final papers that blend firsthand experience with additional research, scholarly resources, and analysis. All three final project options provide equally rigorous academic learning experiences.

## Individual or Group

As you participate in off-campus service-learning opportunities, you may serve individually or with other students. When individual student learning is important, the service is performed independently. For example, the focus of a team-taught course that combines a biology seminar with advanced composition is brain function and attitude development, and the theme is How Do We Know What We Think We Know? There are three options for service-learning community partners: Adopt-a-Grandparent, an organization that supports the developmentally disabled, and an organization that tutors new immigrants. Based on research interests, each student selects one of the three service sites and negotiates the service requested by the community partner to meet his or her learning objectives.

In other service-learning-based courses, the professor may structure the service experience as a group project. Students work in pairs, in small groups, or even as a full class. In an environmental studies class, small groups of two or three students serve at community-based environmental organizations. They participate in field research, restoration, or advocacy work as part of their shared course experience. In a service-learning-based sociology geriatrics course, the entire class participates in a one-time service project at an assisted living center. The students collect oral histories from residents; write, revise, edit, and publish a collection of the stories; and present the publication to the community partner at a social celebration.

While students sometimes gravitate toward individual service work because it provides firsthand experience of how their individual efforts make a difference, group work can greatly affect communities as well. A professor organized the course learning goals of a first-year composition course around the theme of hunger. Throughout the semester, each student served at one of several emergency food distribution sites to learn more about researching and writing about hunger in the community. As individuals, the students made a difference to the hunger agencies in which they served; but at the end of the course, the full class decided to take the new understandings and passion to the broader campus community. The students wanted to go beyond simply participating to transforming their community and the wider world. They mobilized the college campus around Heifer International, a worldwide nonprofit organization that addresses hunger at the grassroots level. Together, the composition class and campus community raised enough money to have an even greater effect than the students had as individuals.

## Short Term or Long Term

Another difference in service-learning experiences is the length of time students serve. In some instances, short-term service provides the learning context, such as when the professor organizes learning goals around a one-time class service experience. In other instances, the service-learning experience involves working at the service site several times. In still other experiences, the service-learning opportunity may run the duration of the course. Sometimes students themselves choose to extend the term of service. Participants recognize the importance of their work and the valuable experiential learning they are gaining, and they look for ways to stay involved.

Whether short term or long term, required or optional, or individual or group, service-learning connects firsthand experience with learning objectives, providing a rich opportunity to serve others and empowering you as a citizen, problem solver, and change maker.

## Direct or Indirect Service

When direct service is incorporated in a course, you will work with the people who use the community partner's services. Each nursing student in a community health nursing course is partnered with a homebound elderly person.

Since the elderly people are unable to regularly visit their doctors and their social stimulation is limited, the student nurses provide regular health checks and companionship. Throughout the semester, they conduct four interviews on nutrition, safety, depression, and what it means to be elderly. The service-learning experience addresses two specific course objectives: to develop patient/client interviewing skills, and to become familiar with the aging process and some related health issues. Through direct one-to-one relationships, these future nurses gain important insights that add to course content. Direct service offers opportunities to see firsthand how your service affects others. For instance, the student nurses witnessed how their personal care and attention improved patient outlook, an important lesson for future nurses.

The immediacy of a direct service relationship may be appealing because of the opportunity to interact on a personal level, often face-to-face. However, the direct approach also presents special challenges. Your social and interpersonal skills may be stretched as you adapt to new situations and individuals. Pre-veterinary science students served at a local humane society, helping with intake, treating foster animals, and providing education and community outreach. Because the people they served changed from week to week, the students were challenged to adapt their interaction and communication styles to suit numerous situations.

With direct service experiences such as this, you will work with individual clients as well as with other volunteers and agency employees. You will be provided with many opportunities to develop effective communication skills, which is not always easy, especially if there are cultural differences. Edward T. Hall, a

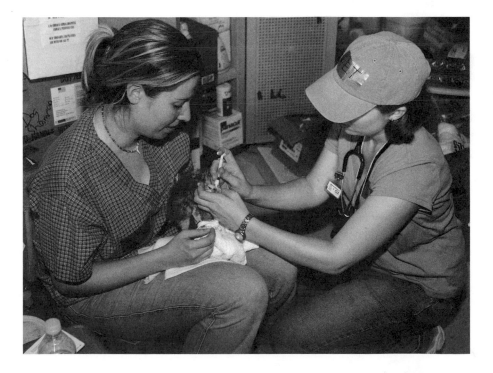

specialist in intercultural communication, developed a theory of communication that depends on what he terms "high-context" and "low-context" (qtd. in LeBaron).

As Jennifer E. Beer explains in "Communicating across Cultures," "High context refers to societies or groups where people have close connections over a long period of time." You are operating in a high-context communication situation when you are with your friends or family. In this context, individuals do not have to be explicit because there is a shared background and a shared understanding of such things as nonverbal cues. If you are familiar with and at ease in the cultural context, you are a high-context communicator.

In contrast, "Low context refers to societies where people tend to have many connections but of shorter duration or for some specific reason. In these societies, cultural behavior and beliefs may need to be spelled out explicitly so that those coming into the cultural environment know how to behave" (Beer). If you come from outside the dominant cultural context and do not share a deep understanding of the situation or the background, you are a low-context communicator. You may find yourself in a low-context situation among people who share a high context when you move from one region of the country to another, such as from the Pacific Northwest to the East Coast. Cultural differences in communication style and understanding necessitate adapting to effectively connect.

In "Communication Tools for Understanding Cultural Differences," Michelle LeBaron uses Hall's theory to create guidelines for operating in a context that varies from one's normative situation:

> Generally, low-context communicators interacting with high-context communicators should be mindful that
> • nonverbal messages and gestures may be as important as what is said;
> • status and identity may be communicated nonverbally and require appropriate acknowledgement;
> • face-saving and tact may be important, and need to be balanced with the desire to communicate fully and frankly;
> • building a good relationship can contribute to effectiveness over time;
> • indirect routes and creative thinking are important alternatives to problem-solving when blocks are encountered.
>
> High-context communicators interacting with low-context communicators should be mindful that
> • things can be taken at face value rather than as representative of layers of meaning;
> • roles and functions may be decoupled from status and identity;
> • efficiency and effectiveness may be served by a sustained focus on tasks;
> • direct questions and observations are not necessarily meant to offend, but to clarify and to advance shared goals; and
> • indirect cues may not be enough to get the other's attention.

As you consider the complex communication context of your service-learning experience, at times you may be the low-context communicator and in other situations you may be the high-context communicator. Regardless of whether you are an insider or an outsider to the dominant cultural context at your service partnership, it may be helpful to keep the simple suggestions in the Tip Box, Communicating with Others, in mind.

## ❗ COMMUNICATING WITH OTHERS

✔ **Respect the community partner, the people it serves, and staff personnel.** Remember that those served and the organization's staff are deeply invested in the agency mission, physical surroundings, and people associated with day-to-day tasks. While serving and learning in their environment, respect the mission, values, and work of the agency. Every individual you encounter deserves to be treated with dignity and respect.

✔ **Maintain confidentiality.** Respect includes maintaining confidentiality. People must trust that you have their best interests at heart, which means, among other things, that you should not casually disclose information about them. You may share stories and information only in the educational context, and even then you should protect the identity of the individuals involved.

✔ **Adjust your communication style.** Identify special information about the site and the individuals you will encounter that you need to understand in order to work effectively in the setting. Practice appropriate speaking and listening for the service situation.

✔ **Listen with your eyes and ears.** Pay attention to your surroundings, observing and listening to interactions at the service site. When people speak to you, focus attentively on them. Guard against merely waiting your turn to speak. Strive to balance talking, listening, and doing, since much is to be gained by all three.

*Online Study Center* college.hmco.com/PIC/duncan1e

## FOCUS EXERCISE

### Identifying Your Communication Context

At your service site, are you a high-context or low-context communicator? Why? Are those you serve high-context or low-context communicators? Why? Depending on your answers, how might you need to adjust your communication style?

Discuss the suggestions identified in the Tip Box. How does each apply to your service site? If necessary, conduct additional research on special communication skills required to work effectively with your community partner. For example, what specialized communication skills are necessary for effective communication with Alzheimer's patients, preschool children, nonnative speakers, or others?

In addition to communication challenges, another potential challenge of direct service is that you may not feel that your service is making a sustainable long-term difference. In other words, although you may feel that you have changed someone's daily life, it may be hard to feel as if your work is making a difference to the larger social issue. For example, political science students who tutor immigrants on U.S. history and government in preparation for the U.S. citizenship exam may question how their effort addresses societal attitudes about immigration. However, active citizenship occurs in many ways and on many levels. At the direct service level, your active participation may cause ripples that you will never see. Your contribution is part of a much larger effort to advocate societal and systemic change for the better. Chapter 3 includes information about different levels of engagement and about how service can move to advocacy on an issue.

A third challenge of direct service is that some participants question whether it is ethical to create a relationship that is not likely to be maintained long term, since the service-learning partnership will conclude at the end of the course. Some service-learning participants feel guilty or regretful when the relationship ends. Be open about the limited time frame of your commitment, and consider extending your service beyond the parameters of your course commitment if doing so is an option. To help reduce your anxiety about departure from a service site, your professor likely will offer strategies to help you leave with diplomacy, appropriate communication, and tact. Also remember that your institution or professor may continue the commitment to the service site by offering other students the opportunity to directly serve and learn there.

Not all service experiences use the direct approach. If your professor and the community partner have decided that indirect service is the best way to incorporate service-learning, your experience will focus less on working directly with individual clients and more on working with the community partner in a broader, more general sense. Indirect service helps build the capacity of an organization to meet its mission. Students do such service work as fundraising, grant writing, and data collection. You may provide a report, a questionnaire, data, or another product that addresses the broader mission of the agency. Had the professor in the community health nursing class previously described incorporated the indirect service-learning approach, the student nurses might have helped write grants to secure additional funding for a nutrition program for the community's home-delivered meal program. Or they may have collected data to assess the needs of the homebound residents.

Indirect service offers opportunities to focus on broad issues central to sustaining the mission and goals of the community partner. While direct service may be appealing because one-to-one relationships potentially enrich the lives of both parties, indirect service helps transform the community at a systemic level.

Whether the service-learning is organized around direct or indirect service, part of your responsibility as an engaged learner is to recognize meaning in the experience. If you are serving in an indirect manner, making meaning may be challenging. Consider Maia, a student who served weekly at a local homeless shelter as part of an economics class. One of the course objectives stipulated that students would investigate the effect of low-wage jobs on survival necessities such as food and clothing. Before going to the shelter, Maia thought that her service would include one-to-one contact with homeless persons, but each week she found herself providing the indirect service of sorting donated clothing. At first she was frustrated by her lack of direct contact and noted this frustration in her reflection journal. Eventually, through reflection, ongoing service, and class discussion, Maia came to appreciate the importance of her service and what she was learning. She began to realize that low-wage income earners could not afford basic clothing. She also noted that those who were living at the shelter and looking for jobs sometimes were hindered by the poor-quality, outdated clothing donated. The experience gave her a new understanding about the economic necessity of charitable shelters, yet made her question the assistance provided by some individuals' giving decisions. Even as Maia challenged accepted notions of giving and learned about economic realities, she also came to realize the importance of her work to the residents and to the homeless shelter. Because of her indirect service in the clothing room, the homeless clients had access to clean, sorted clothing, and the trained agency personnel were able to use their time to conduct other essential work.

One of your challenges as a service-learning participant, regardless of whether you are doing direct or indirect service, is to explore how your service helps the agency as a whole and improves the broader community. Consider these questions:

- Why does the agency need me to do this?

- How does what I do provide time for the staff to do other necessary tasks?

- What difference is the agency making in the larger community, and how does my work help make that happen?

**FOCUS EXERCISE**

**Specifying the Type of Service-Learning in Which You Are Participating**

Reflect on the various types of service-learning about which you have read: required or optional, individual or group, short term or long term, and direct or indirect. Write a brief paragraph articulating how your service-learning experience is constructed and how it fits into the various kinds described in this chapter. Compare your response with someone else involved in the same experience. Did you both reach the same conclusions? Consult with your instructor or facilitator to confirm your conclusion.

# Other Service-Learning Options

Service-learning is a varied pedagogy that may be creatively adapted to many different learning contexts in addition to academic courses, student life organizations, and cocurricular activities. There are specialized movements on campuses that also provide opportunities for service-learning. These include campus-wide initiatives, study abroad, alternative break programs, graduation requirements, and beyond graduation programs.

## Campus-wide Initiatives

Many campuses that have taken on the mission of civic engagement find service-learning instrumental to carrying out their vision for students. They may use such campus-wide initiatives as embedding service-learning into first-year student orientation, which is sometimes called Welcome Week. At Concordia College in Moorhead, Minnesota, incoming students and upper-class peer mentors participate in Hands for Change, which sends groups of fifteen to twenty students to serve community organizations in the metropolitan area for a day. The day begins with contemplation of the service and learning objectives, followed by a sendoff ceremony. Students then work on-site with their community partners. Following the service activities, they reflect on the experience in small-group sessions led by peer mentors and a faculty representative. Finally, the entire group comes back together for a celebration of service.

This is one of many programs across the nation. During Welcome Week at Iowa State University, students participate in such service projects as packaging food for Outreach Africa. At Eastern Michigan University's new student orientation, which is known as Fusion, students spend a day in community service to better connect with both their new campus and the community. When service-learning is implemented during Welcome Week, students benefit from immediate connection to their new community, and the community benefits from teaching students civic engagement so that they can become future leaders. Perhaps you will have the opportunity to exercise your leadership skills by acting as an upper-class mentor during such an orientation to the service-learning experience.

Other campus-wide initiatives geared to creating citizen leaders establish service experiences for anywhere from a week to a month. These activities have different names, such as Urban Plunge and Justice Journey. The crucial element is serving and learning in a reciprocal relationship that will enrich the wider community and teach the students who serve. In 2006 Campus Compact began "a student civic campaign calling upon the talents and energies of students to participate in the renewal of American democracy" ("College Students"). Recognizing the importance of this campaign, the Pew Charitable Trusts provided significant financial support. The Raise Your Voice Campaign involved 300,000 students across 450 U.S. campuses.

## Study Abroad

Life in the twenty-first century requires us to think, learn, and act beyond national borders. Accordingly, the Association of American Colleges and Universities (AACU) has established four goals for today's students:

- Understanding diverse cultures and understanding cultures as diverse
- Developing intercultural skills
- Understanding global processes
- Preparing for citizenship, both local and global (Cornwell and Stoddard 21)

When global learning and service are connected, the ability to meet these goals increases. As Cornwell and Stoddard point out, "One of the corollaries of a world shaped by globalization is that students need to learn about that world and the processes . . . of change and interaction" (30). In fact, the "Study Abroad," "Service-Learning," and "Understanding Global Processes" sections are consecutive in the AACU report because of their clear links. Cornwell and Stoddard articulate the rationale for combining service-learning and study abroad:

> It is instructive for all [students] to learn about such things as the role of the World Bank in other countries, Non-Governmental Organizations (NGOs), and the extraordinary work of grassroots organizations at home and abroad, like the women's cooperative credit societies in India where very poor women learn business principles and raise each others' consciousness about abuse and family planning. . . . Exposure to radically different social formations, standards of living, and approaches to addressing poverty and literacy can help students form more sophisticated and responsible positions on domestic politics. (29–30)

"Domestic politics" can refer to local politics anywhere in the world and, specifically, to politics where one lives. This implies that students who return from service-learning abroad experiences are more likely to make informed decisions and take responsible action at home.

Though service-learning abroad provides incredible experiences, it also comes with a particular challenge. As Cornwell and Stoddard note, "students doing service-learning [abroad] are at risk of making easy judgments both about class values and about U.S. policies" (29). However, with careful preparation, orientation, and ongoing reflection, participants can overcome this challenge.

The benefit of service-learning abroad, when done well, outweighs the risk. As they serve, students learn how they are a part of the wider world and how that wider world is always present in their lives. Cornwell and Stoddard conclude, "Students need to be able to discern, not how distant these world events are from their immediate concerns, but how their immediate concerns have threads which link them—their actions, their votes, their choices as consumers—to these world events" (31). Clearly, participating in a service-learning abroad experience, assuming one is available, can prepare you more fully to live and act in the world.

## Alternative Break Programs

Though you may not have the time or financial ability to take advantage of service-learning abroad, other alternatives that cost less money and take less time also provide rich experiences. These programs are generally referred to as alternative break programs. Many colleges and universities use similar language to describe them:

> An alternative break program places teams of college . . . students in communities to engage in community service and experiential learning during their summer, fall, winter, weekend or spring breaks. Students perform short term projects for community agencies and learn about issues such as literacy, poverty, racism, hunger, homelessness and the environment. The objectives of an alternative break program are to involve college students in community-based service projects and to give students opportunities to learn about the problems faced by members of communities with whom they otherwise may have had little or no direct contact. (Break Away)

Though your college or university may not offer alternative break programs, regional, national, and international agencies provide such experiences. One such agency, Break Away, organized service-learning breaks for some thirty-five thousand students during 2006. The Break Away website describes the relevance of alternative experiences:

> Being completely immersed into diverse environments enables participants to experience, discuss, and understand social issues in a significant way. The intensity of the experience increases the likelihood that participants will transfer the lessons learned on-site back to their own communities even after the alternative break ends. Break Away seeks to use alternative breaks as a springboard into life-long active citizenship . . . where the community becomes a priority in an individual's life decisions.

Recognizing the continued learning and civic engagement opportunities that alternative breaks provide, many college campuses and students have instituted them. For instance, many campuses connect students to Habitat for Humanity through the local chapters and send them to less familiar communities during breaks. Students in the Midwest may head to the Deep South, while Southerners may head to the Northeast. In 2006 Salt Lake Community College students worked with homebound seniors and critically ill citizens in San Francisco as part of Project Open Hand, a service-learning opportunity that focuses on making changes in life choices. Students from Alma College in Michigan went to Golden Pond, Kentucky, to help prepare a national recreational area that expected 2 million

visitors that season. Their learning objectives focused on the natural environment. Monmouth College expresses a vision for these alternative breaks: "We envision in a not too distant future, where quality alternative breaks will be as much a part of the college experience as going to class. Students will walk away with a redefined sense of community and a lifetime commitment to social action" (Wackerle Career and Leadership Center).

## Graduation Requirements

A growing number of higher education institutions are making service-learning a graduation requirement (Enos and Troppe). Centenary College of Louisiana and North Carolina Central University, among other institutions, began requiring service-learning in the 1990s. Since then, many more have joined the movement.

Sometimes the requirement is built into core or general education. For instance, students at Portland State University engage in service-learning in the first-year seminar, in capstone courses, and in a variety of other courses in the curriculum. The initial seminar and the capstone serve as a frame into which the whole college experience fits (Enos and Troppe 67).

Other colleges and universities require a certain number of hours of service-learning, ranging from 30 to 120 depending on the institution. The projects are overseen by a faculty member, a service-learning director, or another campus facilitator. Once a project has been approved and completed, the hours served are recorded on the student transcript. Future employers can thus see that a student has been involved in service-learning, which may cause the employer to

## FOCUS EXERCISE

### Discovering Service-Learning Options on Your Campus

Try to discover current options for service-learning on your campus. If an office, an administrator, or a student organization coordinates service-learning activities, begin there. Ask for a list of service-learning opportunities on campus, and inquire about how to become involved.

If no one place or person coordinates service-learning activity, conduct an informal survey in your dorm or classes under the guidance of your current facilitator. Ask questions that will help you discover how many kinds of opportunities are available and how many students are actively involved.

The key to this focus exercise is to ascertain the breadth and depth of service-learning experiences on your campus. This information can provide a frame within which your experience fits and can lead you to future involvement in other service-learning opportunities.

put that student at the top of the list of prospective employees, a benefit that is discussed and documented in Chapter 4.

## Beyond Graduation

Even after you graduate, there are opportunities to take part in service and make it a learning opportunity. AmeriCorps is a national movement with many branches, all funded federally under the Corporation for National and Community Service. It is "a network of local, state, and national service programs that connects more than 70,000 Americans each year in intensive service to meet our country's critical needs in education, public safety, health, and the environment. AmeriCorps members serve with more than 3,000 nonprofits, public agencies, and faith-based and community organizations" ("What Is AmeriCorps?"). There are two specific branches to which you can apply for a full-time term of service: Ameri-Corps*VISTA (Volunteers in Service to America), and AmeriCorps*NCCC (the National Civilian Community Corps). A person who applies to VISTA should have a college education or three years' work experience.

AmeriCorps provides benefits to those who serve:

> VISTA members who successfully complete a term of service are eligible to receive either an AmeriCorps Education Award or up to $4,725 or an end-of-service stipend. Additional benefits include training, a living allowance, limited health care benefits, relocation expenses, student-loan forbearance or deferment, and non-competitive eligibility. You may also be eligible for childcare assistance should you need it. In addition to these benefits, AmeriCorps*VISTA members learn new skills and acquire qualities of leadership that help prepare them for jobs, and gain a sense of satisfaction from making a significant contribution to their community. (AmeriCorps VISTA)

The NCCC requires a ten-month commitment, during which you would be part of a team-based residential service program in one of five areas: Denver,

**FOCUS EXERCISE**

**Seeking to Serve**

In a small group, brainstorm and discuss ways that you would like to serve if given the opportunity after college. Choose one of the ideas to develop, and do Web research to discover whether organizations or opportunities can directly connect you. Write a short description of a service opportunity that you discovered and that appeals to you. In small groups, share what you have found. Discuss whether you can imagine yourself making such a commitment after college, and why.

Colorado; Charleston, South Carolina; Sacramento, California; Perry Point, Maryland; or Washington, D.C. Members of these teams must be eighteen to twenty-four years of age. Team members perform service focused on strengthening community (AmeriCorps NCCC).

Numerous other organizations also provide service experiences. Some focus on education, such as Teach for America, which asks recent graduates to commit two years to teach in low-income urban or rural public schools. Another possibility is Japanese and Exchange Teaching (JET), an organization funded in Japan that recruits recent college graduates from other nations to serve in Japan by teaching language skills, working on intercultural relations, and/or helping with sports education. Still other organizations affording service experiences beyond college are faith-based initiatives, such as the Lutheran Volunteer Corps:

> a year-long service program for people 21 and over seeking to unite faith, social justice, community living, and simplicity. Volunteers are matched with non-profit organizations in ten metropolitan areas across the United States. They work full-time in various positions ranging from direct social services, to political advocacy, community organizing, education, and activism while living in intentional community.

In short, if you are interested in a continuing commitment to service and learning, there are a wealth of opportunities. Think about where, how, and why you want to serve; then start looking for the way to fulfill that desire.

# Why Do Service-Learning?

# Becoming Good Citizens

**3**

## Preparing to Live as Citizens in Community

An important part of adulthood includes preparing to live as responsible citizens in local, regional, national, and global communal situations. In 2002 the Association of American Colleges and Universities (AACU) published *Greater Expectations: A New Vision for Learning as a Nation Goes to College*. This national panel report, which explores the nature of higher education in the United States, calls for education that "prepares . . . [students] for personal success and fosters a just, democratic society," ensuring that all graduates lead personally fulfilling and socially responsible lives in the workplace and the community (21). According to Fredric A. Waldstein, a political science professor who holds

### LEARNING OBJECTIVES

After studying this chapter and doing the exercises, you should be able to

- Define *public judgment, morals, ethics, polity, the good life, applied contemplation, personally responsible citizenship, participatory citizenship, transforming citizenship, race, class, gender, prejudice, ally*

- Determine the ethics you should practice in community with others

- Recognize the key aspects of Aristotelian citizenship and how they are still relevant today

- Describe the levels of engagement

- Understand the role of service in a participatory democracy

- Create a personal manifesto

- Identify the characteristics of an effective leader

- Identify the qualities of an effective team member

- Recognize and work to overcome stereotypes and assumptions

the Irving R. Burling Chair in Leadership at Wartburg College, "The survival of our democratic system is dependent upon our ability to encourage our students to value democratic engagement in the public sphere. We are, among other things, educating students to lead lives as productive citizens" (71).

As citizens of a democratic society with a republican form of government and a capitalist economic system, we may sometimes feel a conflict between 39 community and individuality. Though we may always experience healthy and creative tension between the two ideals, conflict is not inevitable. No individual can function in isolation; our lives connect us with others. We are born from others; our deaths affect others; and between these two points, we must live positively among others.

As a part of becoming productive citizens, we need to learn "public judgment."[1] According to Waldstein, "Public judgment refers, at least in part, to the capacity of citizens to employ skills of critical inquiry to make informed decisions about that which is in the best long-term interests of the polity at large" (71). In serving and learning from others, we become better able to make productive public judgments based on experience, action, and thoughtful reflection. When individuals are considerate of others, ethical leadership naturally results. While *morals* refer to *personal values that guide an individual's actions*, the more socially constructed *ethics* refers to *accepted moral behavior within groups, communal notions of right and wrong*.

To be truly moral, one must be ethical. Failing to concern themselves with others may afford individuals temporary power and wealth, but it will almost always result in eventual destruction. Such failure of judgment and the resulting destruction was evident when the greed of a few individuals destroyed a once-viable energy corporation known as Enron, resulting in massive job loss and financial ruin for employees and jail terms for those responsible. Had Enron's executives considered the welfare of other people, the corporation might still be strong, and all those involved—from hourly workers to the best-paid executives—might be gainfully employed and happily productive. Imagine the

---

## Five Ethical Leadership Behaviors

- *Be honest and trustworthy, and have integrity in dealing with others.* Consistently tell the truth so that others accept your word. Integrity means also practicing what you preach.

- *Pay attention to all stakeholders.* Treat everyone affected by your decisions and actions—from the top administrator to the least powerful member of your community—with fairness.

- *Build community.* Establish and work together toward common goals.

- *Respect the individual.* Recognize the worth of every individual, and treat each person with courtesy and kindness.

- *Accomplish silent victories.* When leading, use modesty and restraint as well as compromise, when appropriate, to achieve your goals in an ethical fashion.

**Source:** Adapted from Dubrin 168–171.

---

[1] The term comes from Yankelovich. Others, such as Waldstein, have used it in discussions of service-learning and civic literacy.

far-reaching effects—lost homes, broken marriages, shattered confidence, and so much more—that failures of judgment wreak.

When we consider not only ourselves but also the *polity*, or *community body*, we often come upon the vulnerability of others. Philosopher Emmanuel Levinas urges us to see and value other people, especially because we recognize their vulnerability, and to act for their sake rather than behaving in self-centered, isolationist ways that do not reflect our humanity and the reality of our world. Service-learning experiences force us to see the needs of others as well as our own needs. We are called on to respect these people because they, like us, are human and vulnerable.

Recognizing the vulnerability of all human beings is not enough, though it may help us develop compassion. At some point, we need to exercise compassion through action. Action is a responsibility that grows out of citizenship in our country and our world. In *Education for Democracy* Barber and Battistoni declare:

> While service can and does mean many good things, service in a democracy must first of all be seen as a crucial aspect of social responsibility: a model of the relationships between rights-bearing citizens and the many communities to which they belong. To be a citizen is not merely to have rights but to take responsibility, to see ourselves and our interests as flourishing only as our communities flourish. (vii)

For our communities to flourish, we must be willing to serve the interests and needs of our fellow citizens, not simply our own. We must learn to make positive public judgments that reflect moral and ethical standards that take human vulnerability into consideration. Through service-learning, you gain experience in a public arena as you serve others, and that experience will help you make informed judgments even as you are becoming a productive and responsible citizen.

Service-learning can give you opportunities to practice public judgment in service to the community, and therefore give you greater confidence in the role you play in our democracy. In "Voting and Beyond: Engaging Students in Our Representative Democracy," Richard Cone and his colleagues discuss how service-learning "can be designed to unveil and probe the political and policymaking decisions of democratic work. Such efforts can help students better understand how to channel their efforts and tie their commitment to community to political and policy change and to a new view of community" (6).

## FOCUS EXERCISE

### Forming Public Judgment

Brainstorm issues at your school or in the wider local area that are currently in the news or being debated. Which of these issues do you need to learn more about? Plan how to become more informed about the issue so as to reach a positive public judgment. Follow through with the plan, and begin a course of action based on your judgment. Document this entire process, and share it with at least three other people.

For instance, while studying environmental impact policies, Stephanie chose to serve a city commission that was engaged in studying the feasibility of a non-smoking ordinance. The commission had been at work for almost a full year when Stephanie began her service-learning experience. Over the course of the semester, in addition to routine tasks, she carried out research on the failure or success of such ordinances in other cities. She wrote an environmental and economic impact argument that provided essential data for the commission to use in its final considerations. Within six months, the commission reached a decision and publicized Stephanie's research: consequently, the city enacted a non-smoking ordinance. Stephanie received personal thanks from the mayor and city commission, but her greatest reward was seeing her service create political change that benefited the entire community.

Though Stephanie was working and serving with others, she was called on and trusted to work independently as well. Never did the commissioners make her feel that she was subordinate. Rather, they valued her contribution as equal to their own contributions. It is not unusual for the service-learning experience to provide opportunities to accept responsibility and to achieve independence in a setting that treats all citizens equitably. In *Where's the Learning in Service-Learning?* Eyler and Giles cite several studies that indicate that

> The relationship between students and teachers in the classroom is hierarchical; instructors are the authoritative givers of information, and students are the receivers. Moving from the classroom, where they complete assignments for professors, to the field, where they complete real and meaningful work for the community, changes this subordinate role for students; part of the essence of adult citizenship is having important responsibilities. (42)

Because your teacher may not be present at the service-learning site, you must take responsibility for your own learning, judgment, and actions. You directly benefit from the service-learning experience as it gives you the practice you need to assume responsible adult roles.

It is not unusual for students to struggle with the idea that serving the needs of others also benefits themselves. Education professor Robert Rhoads, author of *Community Service and Higher Learning*, records that one student "felt the strain between the ideals of the caring self and those often encouraged by a society centered on competition and a survival-of-the-fittest mentality. Individualism is so pervasive that, even in the context of community service projects, some students still wrestled with whether it was helpful or not to make connections with others" (73).

What we must come to recognize is that, in the truest sense of America's education system, we are freeing ourselves. As Waldstein puts it, "Learning as a process has an emancipatory effect. It encourages one to participate productively in the marketplace of ideas. This, in turn, encourages active participation in the public sphere and can lead to what Carole Pateman defines as participatory democracy, a form of democracy that can transcend politics and permeate all aspects of society" (71).

This notion of participatory democracy is further elaborated in the discussion of your role as a citizen later in this chapter. From the beginning, it is important to realize how service-learning is helping you become a better citizen and a more complete human being. In the words of Megan R., a student who tutored immigrants in the New Americans program: "I'm so thankful for this opportunity to serve others. I've learned so much from it. My site has given me new friends and relationships. It's opened almost another world for me. This opportunity has also shown me no matter how little I think I'm doing, I *am* making a change. I am affecting lives."

# The Value and Virtue of Citizenship

From ancient times, people interested in democratic values have contemplated how to practice individuality while responsibly and productively living in community. Western culture looks to classical Greece, specifically to the city-state of Athens, as the birthplace of democracy. Athenian culture was built on the notion of citizenship. One of its greatest thinkers, Aristotle, wrote of the values and virtues that a person must practice "to discover the good for an individual and a community" (Irwin xvi).

From Aristotle to today's social philosophers, great thinkers have promoted the value and virtue of a thoughtfully active citizenship. Such a citizenship requires us to practice the good life for ourselves and to live well in relationship with others. *The good life* refers to *happiness that results from living a virtuous life*. Through service-learning, you will be practicing the good life for yourself, benefiting from the knowledge and experience your partners provide, and doing good on behalf of community. This active, reciprocal connectedness is key to living well in relationship with others.

**Previewing Key Aspects of Aristotelian Citizenship**

Attaining the good life—the happiness that results from living a virtuous life—requires practicing the following:

- Applied contemplation
- Relationships that promote the welfare of the community
- The building of virtue through habitual practice
- Reverence for equality and social justice
- The practice of generosity in giving and receiving

According to Aristotle, human purpose was to live "a good life guided by practical reason," which led to the notion that human good was "an ACTIVITY of the SOUL[2] in accordance with complete virtue in a complete life." The correlation was that "virtuous activity CONTROLS happiness" (Irwin xvii). First, one cannot lead a good life without profound and careful thought that is practical; contemplation should affect daily decisions and life. We might call this concept *applied contemplation*, which means *thinking that leads to action*. Service-learning lets you apply what you learn from books and in class to real needs in the world; during your service you will need to use practical reasoning to make good decisions.

While serving at the YWCA women's shelter for her child development class, Maren noticed that few activities were planned for weekends, even though there were many families with children of varying ages. She decided to organize a movie night. First, she sought permission from the community partner. Because as many as sixteen children might attend, Maren asked three friends to join her to help watch over the children. She told her friends about the rules of confidentiality that would apply. Maren admits, "Trying to work out a date and setting it all up proved more difficult than I expected. It was almost defeating, but I pressed on." Before selecting the films, she talked with the families to discover what they had seen, what they wanted to see, and what they disliked. She decided to provide cookies and juice for the children. Finally, reasoning that children might have a lot of energy to burn, she and her friends played games with them before showing the films. Maren saw that movie night made a difference in an otherwise dull or trying weekend: "The moms thanked us over and over again. . . . They were so grateful for us spending our time with the kids and giving them something fun and out of the ordinary." The film evenings were successful because Maren used practical reasoning to identify a need, anticipate problems, and organize solutions.

Though Aristotle's understanding of the reasoning process stills works, his concept of the soul may seem markedly different from our own. To classical

---

[2]In Irwin's translation of Aristotle's work, significant terms are capitalized. We have maintained the style of this source.

Greeks, the soul was not limited to the individual. Instead, the soul, which constitutes our humanity, included the other people who influenced a person's life. Classical Greeks understood that people were made up of individual characteristics and of life experiences and that the people with whom they lived shaped them and shared a part of them (Gilmore 11). They understood the importance of both nature and nurture in shaping the soul.

Activity of the soul necessitated activities among people, or living one's citizenship: "For while it is satisfactory to acquire and preserve the good even for an individual, it is finer and more divine to acquire and preserve it for a people and for cities" (Aristotle bk. I, ch. 2, sec. 8). What was the result of such thoughtful work? According to Aristotle, real happiness (a state of being rather than a passing moment of pleasure) was controlled by the actions people undertook as they lived the good life on the basis of sound thinking. We can apply Aristotle's teachings to an overarching benefit of service-learning: that we will be better, happier people both individually and in community.

Addressing how to build a virtuous character through habituating oneself to live a good life, Aristotle wrote: "We become just by doing just actions, temperate by doing temperate actions, brave by doing brave actions" (bk. II, ch. 1, sec. 4). He defined *just* as "whatever produces and maintains happiness and its parts for a political community" (bk. V, ch. 1, sec. 13), again emphasizing the importance of the entire citizenry. He also referred to justice as the "complete virtue" and urged people who had more to work toward equality by giving more: "There would be no community without exchange, no exchange without equality" (bk. V, ch. 5, sec. 14).

Clearly Aristotle understood that a healthy community, which results in happiness for all, depends on a reverence for equality and social justice. When someone in the community is in need, meeting that need will help everyone in the community. When you attend to community needs through service-learning, not only do the receivers of the service benefit, but you also benefit by what you learn in the process and by gaining a healthier society in which you and others can happily live.

Finally, Aristotle identified generosity as one of the specific virtues that helped create the virtuous character and, thus, a socially just society:

> Using wealth seems to consist in spending and giving, whereas taking and keeping seem to be possessing rather than using. That is why it is more proper to the generous person to give to the right people than to take from the right sources. . . . For it is more proper to do good than to receive good . . . and clearly giving implies doing good and doing fine actions, while taking implies receiving well or not doing something shameful. (bk. IV, ch. 1, sec. 7–8)

Most of us have heard that "it is better to give than to receive," but we too often take pride in giving to others but remain unable to graciously receive anything from another person. Aristotle's words admonish us to be generous in our giving, but also to do well in receiving. As you interact with others through service-learning, you will be called on to give of your wealth—your energy, time, and talents—and also to look for and be open to what you are receiving from the people and the experience. The notion of the rightness of the giving connects with creating partnerships through which we receive learning from agencies that practice good for others and are in need of what we have to give.

# Service-Learning in the Aristotelian Tradition

Greek democracy and Aristotelian philosophy continues to influence American society today. Our philosophers, sociologists, political scientists, and educators continue to think, write, and act on the role of the individual within community, the virtue and value of citizenship. In *Soul of a Citizen: Living with Conviction in a Cynical Time*, Paul Rogat Loeb insists that "public participation is the very soul of democratic citizenship" (2). To enjoy the benefits of democracy, we should participate in the public sphere and work to improve the lives of other citizens. If Aristotle is right that we need to practice virtue, we need to be educated about citizenship and practice our participatory responsibility. Service-learning affords us the opportunity to learn how to participate and to grow as citizens. Colleges that seriously implement service-learning for the sake of students and the wider community are helping produce people more prepared to live productive and meaningful lives.

In their reflection on the value of service-learning to education and to a student's future in the world, national service-learning consultants James and Pam Toole conclude that "There was a direct and vigorous connection between the character of the students' education and their present and future role as democratic citizens" (110). Some people may feel that students need only classroom experience to be fully educated, productive citizens. However, our world demands more than theoretical knowledge or even knowledge gained from well-controlled laboratory experiments. As Robert A. Rhoads indicates, "The values of the heart—concern for the common good, a sense of compassion, courage to seek justice, devotion to one's community—all require a sense of connection to others which a completely abstract education cannot provide" (92). When you are engaged in service-learning, you are actively demonstrating your concern for the common good and devotion to community in the Aristotelian tradition. You exercise compassion and courage for the sake of justice, for the sake of others. You are learning how to live and act in a just, democratic society.

With its ongoing interest in keeping faith with the democratic ideals on which the nation was founded, the U.S. government underscores the importance of connecting service with education. One national program that emphasizes that connection is AmeriCorps. In their book on the keys to educational success, Figler and his colleagues observe that "The government has made an effort to stress the importance of community service as part of what it means to be a good citizen, and it provides support for that effort through AmeriCorps. AmeriCorps provides financial awards for education in return for community service work" (262). Students often apply to AmeriCorps on graduating from college, and service-learning experience while in college shows that they are serious about the role of service in community. Teachers who implement service-learning in their classes are supporting a national effort and are preparing students to take their place as responsible citizens who carry out the ideals of our society. Since you are participating in service-learning, you are well placed to move forward in society and to continue to benefit from the contributions that you and others have made.

Of course, you may reach this point of contemplating the significance of service-learning but feel that you have enough to do to balance coursework, jobs, cocurricular activities, and family. You may feel that service is something you can do later, when you are established in a career and financially secure. You may even feel that such work is better done, perhaps can only be done, by extraordinary people or highly successful people who have few pressures in their daily lives. Not everyone can be as saintly as Mother Teresa or Nelson Mandela or as generous as Bill and Melinda Gates or Warren Buffet. Perhaps it is easier for the individuals who use their fame and success to help others than it would be for us: people like singer Paul Hewson, known as Bono in the band U2, who has worked tirelessly in the cause of confronting HIV/AIDS in Africa, and actress Angelina Jolie, who was appointed Goodwill Ambassador for the United Nations High Commissioner for Refugees because of her work in Asia and Africa.

First, not all famous and successful people contribute. Numerous famous and successful individuals behave poorly and demonstrate poor character and judgment: "For without virtue it is hard to bear the results of good fortune suitably" (Aristotle bk. IV, ch. 3, sec. 21). Second, all of us are capable of serving in some way and will benefit richly from what we learn in the process.

Loeb recognized the tension between wanting to do good and thinking that others are better positioned to act. In response, he wrote *Soul of a Citizen*, an insightful and well-documented book that portrays ordinary people who actively serve their communities, seeking out needs, discovering that they can help, and describing how much they learn and grow in the process. Loeb writes of Virginia Ramirez, a woman with an eighth grade education. Following the death of an elderly woman from cold in an unheated home, Ramirez realized that poor Hispanic neighborhoods in San Antonio, Texas, were not being dealt with equitably by local government. Working with Communities Organized for Public Service (COPS), she found evidence of misspent public funds. Eventually, the San Antonio city council reallocated funds to the Hispanic neighborhood so that homes could be repaired and lives saved (Loeb, *Soul* 15–20).

Hearing how other ordinary people serve may help you realize that you can act now and that your actions will have results. As Loeb puts it, "We need to believe that our individual involvement is worthwhile, that what we might do in the public sphere will not be in vain" (3). In describing the many ordinary people who do good, Loeb could be describing what you will gain through service-learning:

> [Those] who get involved view their place in the world very differently. They have learned specific lessons about approaching social change: that they don't need to wait for the perfect circumstances, the perfect cause, or the perfect level of knowledge to take a stand; that they can proceed step by step, so that they don't get overwhelmed before they start. They savor the journey of engagement and draw strength from its challenges. Taking the long view, they come to trust that the fruits of their efforts will ripple outward, in ways they can rarely anticipate. (8–9)

Sometimes you need to set aside your apprehension, or even cynicism, and make an effort in order to discover how much you can accomplish and learn through simple acts of service. With enough practice, service becomes a good habit, a part of the good life.

# Levels of Engaged Citizenship

At different stages of your life and with regard to various issues, you may practice different levels of engaged citizenship. You may act as a personally responsible citizen, a participatory citizen, or a transforming citizen.[3] People at each of the three levels respond differently to social issues, such as the issue of hunger. Examine the table below to see how this example plays out for the different citizens at different stages.

---

[3]These terms and ideas come from Westheimer and Kahne, whose ideas were adapted by Toole. We have made grammatical changes in Toole's table and have reversed two of the columns: Sample Action and Description.

## Levels of Engagement

| TYPE OF CITIZEN | CORE ASSUMPTION | DESCRIPTION | SAMPLE ACTION | CIVIC KNOWLEDGE |
|---|---|---|---|---|
| **Personally Responsible Citizen** | Citizenship involves being a good, responsible, law-abiding member of the community. | • Works and pays taxes<br>• Obeys laws<br>• Votes<br>• Recycles, gives blood<br>• Lends a hand in time of crisis | Contributes to a food drive | • Exercises compassion and social responsibility |
| **Participatory Citizen** | Citizenship involves active participation and leadership in the community to help improve the quality of life for all. | • Participates in community organizations and/or improvement efforts<br>• Organizes community efforts to care for people in need, promotes economic development, cleans up environment, supports the arts | Helps organize a food drive | • Knows how public sector (government, nonprofit groups) works<br>• Knows strategies for accomplishing tasks<br>• Organizes and motivates others |
| **Transforming Citizen** | Citizenship involves a responsibility to question and change the system when it is unjust or ineffective. | • Critically assesses social, political, and economic structures to see beyond surface causes<br>• Educates others and forms partnerships on community issues<br>• Acts to change areas of injustice through policy and social innovation | Explores why people are hungry and acts to solve root causes | • Knows how to analyze and effect systemic change<br>• Knows about social movements<br>• Has courage to take a stand different than other people's<br>• Is action-oriented |

**Source:** Toole. Adapted from Westheimer and Kahn.

**Personally responsible citizenship** involves being a good, responsible, law-abiding member of the community. This type of citizen is compassionate and socially responsible. Such a person works and pays taxes, obeys laws, votes, recycles, gives blood, and lends a hand in a time of crisis, such as by contributing to a food drive. We hope that all of us are personally responsible citizens all the time. However, sometimes we may not practice responsible citizenship; perhaps we drive faster than the posted speed limit or when we have had too much to drink. We all know that driving under the influence of alcohol is irresponsible, but people may not always practice practical reasoning and good decision making. If you are not yet at the level of personal responsibility, service-learning may help you get there.

**Participatory citizenship** involves active participation and leadership in the community to help improve the quality of life for all. The participatory citizen knows how the public sector works, knows strategies for accomplishing collective tasks, and is a good organizer and motivator. Such a person is an active member of community organizations and/or improvement efforts. This type of citizen will organize efforts to care for those in need, such as a food drive, will promote economic development, will clean up the environment, and will support the arts. Virginia Ramirez became a participatory citizen when she joined COPS. The action portion of service-learning is designed to change a responsible citizen into a participatory citizen.

**Transforming citizenship** involves taking responsibility to question and change an unjust or ineffective system. The transforming citizen knows how to analyze and effect systemic change, knows about social movements, has the

courage to take a stand different from the stands of other people, and is action-oriented. This individual knows which key organizations and decision makers can help effect change. This person critically assesses social, political, and economic structures to see beyond surface causes; educates others and forms partnerships around a deeper view of community issues; and acts to change injustice through policy and social innovation. When it comes to the hunger issue, the transforming citizen explores why people are hungry and acts to solve root causes. Through the contemplation and reflection aspects of service-learning, which are discussed in Chapter 6, we hope to move you toward becoming transforming citizens. Concrete experience and thoughtful reflection help reveal underlying causes, who can effect change, and how to pursue policy solutions. Because service-learning requires depth of thought about the experience and related issues, it can help you become a transforming citizen.

# A Personal Case of Engagement

Service and learning provide the core that creates good citizens. As you move forward in life, you will be better prepared to judge whether you can and should operate at each of the civic engagement levels. To show how engagement levels shift over time or with different situations, Dawn Duncan, one of the authors of this text uses reflection to directly explain her levels of civic engagement.

---------------

I look at my life now and see that I am a **personally responsible citizen** most of the time, though I confess to occasionally speeding to a meeting. As a **participatory citizen**, I work with my church and the college where I teach to address various needs, differing in different semesters depending on the needs of the community and my students. I have helped build Habitat for Humanity homes, spent time improving American Indian reservations, volunteered at a local food pantry, and worked with the elderly in nursing homes. As a **transforming citizen**, I have focused on two areas: the arts and peace. As president of a nonprofit community theatre, I helped draft a new mission and corresponding aspects of the theatre to meet the needs of our community. Now many people who never had access to theatre productions because of economic or physical hardship can both attend and participate in productions.

So that you do not think my level of engagement is all about service as action and does not include learning, it is important for me to stipulate that I am learning all the time. For instance, the artistic director and the development director of the community theatre helped me rethink how to motivate a new board of directors, the role of the board in fundraising, and what the theatre could economically and structurally achieve.

Finally, I needed to both learn and serve in the area of peace activism. Fortunately, our campus provides a wonderful cocurricular opportunity for faculty, students, and the wider community by regularly hosting the Nobel Peace Prize Symposium. During the 2003 symposium, Ambassador Anwarul K. Chowdhury, UN undersecretary-general and high representative for the least developed countries, landlocked developing countries, and small island developing states, spoke on building a culture of peace. The ambassador, who for decades had worked in some of the most dismal conditions and stressful situations, challenged each of us to find a way to use our particular gifts to serve the world. He emphasized that each person can and does make a difference in the world, and the idea was most compelling because he is not a naïve idealist but rather someone who knows and understands the most daunting challenges facing our world. I was inspired—actually compelled—by what I heard to try to meet his challenge.

Here is how I went about trying to meet the challenge. First, I had to take stock of my own abilities and gifts. I think my chief abilities are related to words—understanding their power, choosing how to use them to express myself and connect with others, making them perform and transform through writing and speaking. Next, I needed to think about the world's needs and how my gifts could help meet them. In a time when political pundits and news personalities engage in shouting matches rather than meaningful dialogue, I am increasingly concerned about a breakdown in communication that can only lead to greater societal problems. How then to act and live in order to serve society and use my particular gifts? I decided to write a manifesto as a transformative act and to share the manifesto with family, friends, colleagues, students, and organizations that could and would hold me accountable. Take a few minutes to read my manifesto.

## Words Made Manifest

### Preamble

From the time that some of us were children, we were taught that "sticks and stones may break my bones, but words will never hurt me." Even as children many of us understood that this saying falsely represents reality. Words can do great harm. They can injure emotionally and psychically; they can even initiate physical injury and compel death. The spoken or written word of one in authority holds sway over our lives. But while words have the power to harm, they also have the power to heal. They can bind up our emotional and psychic wounds, inspiring confidence; they can initiate forgiveness or reprieve and foster peace.

*continued*

Because the reality of our lives demonstrates the power of words, we must choose carefully in what way we will make words manifest. Words either harm or heal; they are never neutral. This manifesto is written for those who choose to make manifest the healing power of words in our world. Each of us as individuals must choose whether we can adopt such a manifesto, so the written form of the document that follows will adopt a first-person point of view in order to allow each of us to individually consider this calling to commitment. It is not my place to police the words made manifest in your life. It is my place to carefully consider what I believe I am called to do and to explicitly act on that calling, to try to make manifest words of healing in our world through my life. I invite you to listen, to consider, and, if you are called to do so, to adopt this manifesto for yourself.

## Listening Made Manifest

Before children can understand the meaning and power of words, they must learn how to listen. Listening teaches us what things mean, what certain people mean when they use certain words. In order that I may learn to speak well and wisely, I must first learn to listen well.

1. Whether I am listening to spoken, signed, or written words, **I must be present in the moment and attentive** to the author of those words.

2. Though to every listening experience I bring my unique self and the shape of my personal experiences, I must consciously attempt to cease being self-centered. I should not merely hear words without listening, an indication that I am merely waiting for my chance to speak. Rather, **I should listen with an eager anticipation** about what I may hear from the author.

3. I should not enter a listening attitude with preconceived notions about the author or about what I may hear, a condition that will cause me to hear only what I want or expect to hear. Rather, **I should listen openly and consider quietly, trying to genuinely understand** what the author is trying to say.

4. I should not impute motives where none have been made explicit, an attitude that may lead to suspicion. Rather, **I should practice generosity in my attitude** toward the author.

5. When I fail to understand, whether due to a lack of information or to a positional difference, I should not become defensive or go on the attack. Rather, **I should seek clarification with honesty and gentleness, with a willingness to learn more** as I listen.

6. I should not be unaware of my body as an expression of my listening attitude; nor should I use my body as a speaking tool, a practice that detracts from listening and distracts the author and other listeners. Rather, **I should practice a receiving attitude in my bodily posture and through my facial expressions**.

7. When the act of listening will create more harm than healing, I should not continue to place myself in a situation that will demand the continuation of such a listening experience. Rather, **I should seek to avoid encouraging harmful speech by not providing myself as a listener** to such speech.

*continued*

8. When I disagree with the words spoken by another, I should not demean the author. Rather, **I should withhold words of attack** and **keep silence when silence has greater power to heal**. When words must be made manifest to create healing where harm has been done, I should have the courage to speak words of healing, for that too is a part of this calling.

## Speech Made Manifest

Once I have come to recognize that words make meaning and that we join in making meaning by speaking to one another, I must consider what I should say and how I might say it. If I am going to take my place in the world community, I have a responsibility to speak healing words.

1. Whenever I speak, **I should always be aware that the words I speak impact others** either negatively or positively. However, currying favor should not be the motivation for my words.

2. **I should choose precisely the words that best communicate** what I wish to express. Sloppiness in word choice can lead to misunderstanding.

3. **I should exercise ambiguity only when it creates greater openness in communication or, conversely, provides safety in harmful situations**. There are times when ambiguity can allow for better dialogue, deeper consideration, more open attitudes. There are also occasions when one's safety might be threatened and only ambiguity will save one from harm. These occasions are not to be confused with manipulating ambiguity for falseness, saving one's self from the consequences of one's own wrong actions.

4. **I should strive to use words that are both honest and positive, healing words**. My words should act as a blessing to the receivers rather than as a curse. Cursing, jokes at the expense of others, denigrating others are all harmful manners of speech.

5. **I should use humor that diffuses hostility and creates moments of delightful laughter**. To this end, I will avoid humor based on otherness and choose self-deprecating humor born of my own life-experience.

6. **I should speak in tones and at a volume that encourages listening**. Shouting causes listeners to cease listening, and whispering always excludes. Those particular volume levels should be exercised rarely, and only when necessary and helpful (e.g., a warning, a brief explanation while someone else is speaking if a nearby listener is confused).

7. **I should ask questions that point toward greater clarity and learning**. The questioning process should always be practiced for beneficial instruction, my own and that of others. Never should questions be posed in order to ridicule, divide, or create harm.

8. **I should speak as if I believe words have life, respecting their power**. Every word springs forth from the womb of the mind and is born into the communal world, acting on that world and rippling forward with effects beyond the locality of the author. I should take care to bring forth healthy words, aware of the privilege I have to bring such life into the world, loving the special qualities of individual words and how they combine to make meaning.

| ISSUE, CAUSE, OR UNDERLYING ISSUES | LIFE SKILLS TO DEVELOP | CONCRETE STEPS TO TAKE |
|---|---|---|
| Self-centeredness | Other-centeredness | Practice being present and attentive to others. |
| Failure to listen to others | Effective listening skills | Eagerly, quietly, and openly listen. |
| False assumptions about others | Generosity of spirit | Do not impute motives; practice generosity, be willing to learn. |
| Socially inappropriate language use or communication style | Effective and positive speaking skills and body language | Choose precise words; speak in appropriate tone and volume; use humor appropriately. |

This manifesto is an example of how a person can move from responsible citizenship to transforming citizenship. To write this manifesto, Duncan had to ask difficult questions about the power of words and the communicative act. A graphic organizer may help clarify the process she went through to create the manifesto.

Duncan felt responsible for exercising practical reasoning as she thought through the issue of communication. She needed to analyze communication acts and critically assess what it would take to achieve communication with the power to affect the world positively and bring about healing. At a participatory level, sharing the manifesto in classes, with civic groups, and through writing allows her to educate others and ask them to think about and act on these commitments to use words responsibly. Of course, she also attempts to enact what she has theorized. As a result, she is transformed even as she acts as an agent of transformation.

# Leadership, Conflict Resolution, and Teamwork

Learning how to become a productive citizen who serves for the greater good of the community naturally prepares you to take leadership roles. The ancient notion that the best leader is a servant holds true today. The servant puts other people first, attending to their needs. The Greenleaf Center for Servant-Leadership, which is based on the work of Robert Greenleaf during the 1970s, defines the concept this way:

> Servant-Leadership is a practical philosophy which supports people who choose to serve first, and then lead as a way of expanding service to individuals and institutions. Servant-leaders may or may not hold formal leadership positions. Servant-leadership encourages collaboration, trust, foresight, listening, and the ethical use of power and empowerment.

*Online Study Center* college.hmco.com/PIC/duncan1e

### FOCUS EXERCISE

#### Creating a Personal Manifesto

Duncan was deeply concerned about the misuse of communication and the harm such misuse causes. Identify a social aspect that deeply concerns you because of a value you hold dear. What are the underlying issues surrounding the problem? What life skills do you need to address these issues? How will these skills translate into concrete action? Use the graphic organizer to critically think through the issues and your response.

| ISSUE, CAUSE, OR UNDERLYING ISSUES | LIFE SKILLS TO DEVELOP | CONCRETE STEPS TO TAKE |
|---|---|---|
| | | |
| | | |
| | | |
| | | |

Now write a personal manifesto that will show you how to develop these skills and take the steps you have indicated. How might you actualize your manifesto in your personal and professional life? For example, Duncan has shared her statement with family, friends, colleagues, and organizations with which she works so that they may hold her accountable, which also creates change in their relationships and in the various organizational settings. Sometimes people who have read "Words Made Manifest" have elected to live by its standards. How can you encourage others to get involved in helping address the social issue you have identified?

Since the 1970s, others have followed Greenleaf's lead and have promoted the concept in the public and private sectors. According to promotional information on the cover of a popular book, James Autry's *The Servant Leader: How to Build a Creative Team, Develop Great Morale, and Improve Bottom-Line Performance*, "one third of the companies on *Fortune*'s '100 Best Companies to Work For' list" practice servant-leadership.

Autry indicates that "Five Ways of Being" are necessary to a good leader: **be authentic, be vulnerable, be accepting, be present**, and **be useful** (10). In the mid-1990s a group of educators collaborated to develop a guidebook on leadership. That guide, now in its fourth edition, establishes a model of leadership known as the "Seven C's": **consciousness of self, congruence** (consistency between belief and action, or integrity), **commitment, collaboration, common purpose, controversy with civility**, and **citizenship**

(Astin 21). These two lists can be integrated. If you are authentic, your behavior will have congruence because you will act as you think, feel, and believe. People with whom you work will be more likely to respond and to trust you when you are authentic. If you are truly conscious of self, you will know and acknowledge your own weaknesses, which make you vulnerable and more human. As discussed earlier, vulnerability is a human condition that connects you with those you serve. To be present to others requires commitment as well as collaboration. Others are counting on you to be where you should be at the arranged time, with your focus on those with whom you are working. To truly be useful, you need to understand the common purpose you share with others. The Seven C's go a step beyond the Five Ways of Being in that they also invoke the citizenship role, including how to handle controversy with civility.

As you serve with your community partner, keep the Five Ways of Being and the Seven C's in mind. Think about how to integrate these attributes of leadership in your service-learning situation.

As indicated by the Seven C's notion of controversy with civility, one mark of good leadership is the ability to negotiate conflict resolution. Conflicts may arise between an administrator and you or a client, between a client and you, between two or more clients, between you and a coworker, and even between you and your instructor or fellow classmates. Though you may consider another party in the conflict to have greater authority than you, you can exercise leadership if you understand how to achieve conflict resolution in community with others. Take a look at the Community Model for Conflict Resolution box.

The first conflict style, avoidance, may work in the short term in certain situations. If someone around whom you work is consistently aggressive or violent, avoiding that person would certainly be beneficial. Taking the passive approach of avoidance may help reduce the potential for violent outbreaks. However, compromise often does not work, since everyone is likely to feel shortchanged by the decision.

The opposite of avoidance, confrontation, is also called for at times. If the behavior of someone around you may lead to a serious situation, even endangerment, you may have to confront that individual. The person causing the difficulty might be unaware of any problem. Perhaps a coworker in a daycare center roughhouses with some of the young children, swinging them by their arms or tossing them into the air. This individual may be unaware of the fragility of young limbs that are still growing, or perhaps he cannot imagine what

# FOCUS EXERCISE

## Distinguishing Quality Leadership

In a small group, discuss your personal experiences with leaders you have admired. Brainstorm your own list of qualities that distinguish effective leadership. How might you practice these leadership qualities during your service-learning experience? How might you practice them on campus and in your personal life?

# Community Model for Conflict Resolution

## Three Basic Conflict Styles

- Avoidance
- Confrontation
- Problem-solving

*Active Listeners*

1. Listen politely.
2. Ask questions for clarification.
3. Repeat what was said in your own words.
4. Summarize.
5. Acknowledge speaker's point of view, feelings, etc.

*Problem-Solving*

1. Choose an appropriate time and place.
2. Identify the problem.
3. Brainstorm solutions.
4. Agree on a solution.
5. Avoid compromise or win/lose situations.
6. Always try for win/win situations.
7. Respect the rights and values of others.
8. Check back later to ensure the solution is working.

**Source:** Rattray.

could happen if he doesn't catch a child. Clearly, compromise would not work in such a situation. To avoid injury to the children, you may be forced to confront your coworker.

In most cases, instead of using compromise or confrontation, you should work together to arrive at a single best answer to the situation. To maximize the opportunity for a solution, active listening should precede the attempt at resolution. Active listening is essential to effective conflict resolution.

The best conflict resolution style for long-term effect is problem solving. Problem solving requires working with others for the best overall outcome. It necessitates respecting and valuing the ideas of others so that the best solution can be agreed on. For example, computer science students who were fulfilling their service-learning with Computer Support Services on campus met a need by taking a leadership role in a situation that called for problem solving. Computer Support Services did not have the time or personnel to pick up computers in need of repair and to deliver them when the repairs were finished. College staff and students had to physically disconnect their computers and transport them to Computer Support Services when repairs were necessary. This became a source of contention. The service-learning students suggested as part of their service commitment that they would set aside time on Tuesdays for pickup and Thursdays for deliveries. The problem was solved to everyone's satisfaction.

When working with groups of people, as you will necessarily be doing when you are serving in community, you will need to become effective at team building. Perhaps you will be part of a class team that serves at the same site, or perhaps you will be working on-site in team situations. Either way, you will be called on to collaborate to achieve the desired goals. At times you may need to take the lead, and at other times you may need to step aside and let others lead. Sometimes there is no discernible leader in a team that is working smoothly with tasks equally distributed. In *When Teams Work Best: 6,000 Team Members and Leaders Tell What It Takes to Succeed*, Frank LaFasto and Carl Larson identify the factors that make for effective teams. Take a moment to study "Six Factors That Distinguish Effective Team Members."

LeFasto and Larson refer to the first two factors as "working knowledge" factors (5) and to the last four as "teamwork factors" (8). Though you may think that you do not have much **experience**, if you have taken careful stock of your skills and abilities, you will know how to use them in a given situation; you will gain experience as you work. **Problem solving** is a critical thinking skill. A working knowledge of problem solving will enable you to adapt to situations as they arise as well as help you think about long-term solutions.

To solve problems, you must remain open to the input of others. LeFasto and Larson single out **openness** as "the basic ingredient for team success" (8). As a team member who encourages teamwork, you should be straightforward and willing to bring up issues that need discussion. You should express your point of view and opinions clearly and provide feedback to your team members. Someone who is closed can negatively affect the team. The closed person acts defensively, does not seek input from others, resists trying new ideas, does not handle confrontation well, and perhaps does not speak up or share ideas (9).

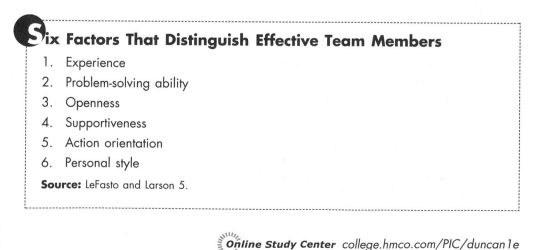

# Six Factors That Distinguish Effective Team Members

1. Experience
2. Problem-solving ability
3. Openness
4. Supportiveness
5. Action orientation
6. Personal style

**Source:** LeFasto and Larson 5.

**Supportiveness** and **action orientation** are self-explanatory. LeFasto and Larson encourage a positive **personal style**. An effective team style includes exhibiting a positive attitude and a sense of joy in your work. Your energy and enthusiasm will become infectious, motivating others. Your friendliness will make others feel comfortable and will help you get along well with them; you will be well-liked. These attributes make it easier for you to share new ideas and exercise creativity.

A negative style is marked by overcompetitiveness, a closed attitude that makes others hesitate to approach you, a cynical and/or impatient nature, and a tendency to be argumentative. Such a style is seen as unfriendly and counterproductive (LeFasto and Larson 23). While it may not always be easy to practice a positive personal style, it is well worth trying because it will make you more effective.

Even though you practice a positive style, others around you may not. You may feel unappreciated or be tempted to adopt the negativity that is directed toward you. If you realize that you will face such challenges, you can be more prepared. Staying positive can be hard work.

In your service-learning situation, you will likely be working with numerous people. Try to think of each person as part of your team. Consciously practice the factors of effective team building, and note the responses of others to you. The more you practice, the more joy and success you and those with whom you work are likely to experience.

# Avoiding Stereotypes, Acknowledging Privilege, and Embracing Diversity

American society has become increasingly complex both because of the variety of people who live here and because of our connections with others around this world. Sociologist Peter Kivisto points out that contemporary society is "considerably more ethnically diverse . . . [as well as] more interconnected and interdependent . . . . We live in a world that is at once local and global" (1).

Because you live in social contact with others and are committing to serve people through your community partnership, you need to recognize social barriers

that may interfere with or cause problems during your service experience. Some of these challenges include ability issues, sexual orientation, nationality/first-language, race, class, and gender. While all are serious concerns and pervasive problems, the last three are the focus of the discussion that follows.

## Race

Working definitions of *race, class*, and *gender* help us recognize the difficulties and engage ideas about how to overcome them. Biology has shown that race is a social reality, not a biological reality. In other words, *race is shared societal understandings about what physical differences mean*. These understandings shift in different times and places. In the nineteenth and early twentieth centuries, immigrants from Ireland and southern and eastern European countries—who today are considered "white"—were considered "non-white." They were portrayed as being racially inferior and were victims of job and housing discrimination. Historian Ronald Takaki, an expert in ethnic studies, explains that race is what one group determines for another in an exercise of power and control. Others inscribe race on us.

Ethnicity, which is often associated with race, can be a matter of choice (Takaki). A person may self-identify as *Irish*-American, but this choice of identity may also cause others to make assumptions. These assumptions lead to stereotyping, making assumptions about an entire group of people based on a singular and often faulty notion. Some stereotypes label people as being prone to violence, extreme sexuality, alcohol or drug dependence, or even lack of a work ethic. According to Kivisto, "In order to avert intercommunal conflict

## FOCUS EXERCISE

### Breaking Down Social Barriers

Select some ethnic part of your genealogical heritage. If you are uncertain about your heritage, focus on what it means to be American or from your region of the country (Southern, Midwestern). If your heritage is mixed, as for most Americans, choose one ethnicity. What stereotypes are associated with this ethnicity? List both positive and negative aspects. Which of these stereotypes might cause social or other difficulties for people of this ethnicity? Conduct research to discover whether this ethnic group ever faced discrimination.

based on ethnic differences, a shared sense of citizenship must be sufficiently powerful to override the divisive potential of ethnic group allegiances" (22). While serving others, you need to recognize that all of us are part of this society and are connected in community, and all deserve to be treated with dignity.

## Class

Racial and ethnic stereotyping can combine with oversimplifying notions of class behavior. Though we may like to imagine that the United States is a classless society, "Class is a hidden reality of American history" and "Race is tied intricately to class. When we understand this intricate tie that binds us, we begin to see that we do share much common ground in class" (Takaki, qtd. in Halford). *Class* involves *shared, socially constructed concepts of how careers and wealth determine behavior.*

One harmful stereotype is the assumption that intelligence is equated with financial wherewithal. The economically advantaged have access to better educational opportunities and to health care that can affect mental capacity, but they are not inherently more intelligent than are people with less financial security. As you work with others, credit their intellectual capacity and try to avoid making false assumptions about their work ethic. The walls of class may not always be visible in this age of informal clothing styles, but we still need to recognize the barriers and work to remove them.

## Gender

When it comes to gender barriers, we often think of glass ceilings rather than invisible walls. *Gender* refers to *socially shared notions about what people of one sex can and should do predicated on a concept of significant differ-ence in capabilities and function based on sex.* Sex is biological, but gender is socially constructed.

Gender roles differ from culture to culture, an important point when liv-ing and working in a multicultural society such as ours. Even within a group that is seemingly racially or ethnically homogenous, gender roles can vary be-cause of class or religious assumptions. As you work with others at your service site, recognize that you may encounter notions about gender roles that differ from your ideas. Try to be aware of your own assumptions and sensitive to the gender attitudes of others. At times you may need to use some of your problem-solving skills to overcome gender prejudices.

## Overcoming Stereotypes

To dismantle barriers, overcome stereotypes and dignify the diverse people you encounter. First, you must desire the same freedoms and dignity for oth-ers as you do for your family and yourself. Accepting the value of all citizens and all guests enriches the national community. "Multiculturalism is an affirm-ing of what this country stands for: opportunity, equality, and the realization of our dream" (Takaki, qtd. in Halford).

Second, examine your assumptions. Once you clearly know what you as-sume, you can begin to question your assumptions and make a concerted effort to set them aside as you work and serve. Becoming aware of your own thoughts and feelings and challenging them will help you begin to erase personal *preju-dice*, which means *a prejudgment of an individual you do not know based on your concepts of external describers* such as race, class, and gender.

The third step is to begin to dismantle systemic or institutional barriers. Do-ing so calls for becoming increasingly aware of how power is exercised over in-dividuals by institutions such as government, business, and social organizations based on these shared social concepts. According to Kivisto, "Reducing levels of prejudice and discrimination are not ends in themselves, but rather should be seen as prerequisites to civic incorporation" (35). In other words, our goal should be a society in which all citizens are equally incorporated into the fabric of society, with each recognized as essential and valuable to the whole. Kivisto dreams of the day citizenship becomes "an overarching mode of identity and basis for social

**FOCUS EXERCISE**

**Becoming Aware of Your Own Barriers**

Reflect on your own assumptions and stereotypes about race, class, gender, ability issues, sexual orientation, first language, nationality/citizenship, and religion. Focus on one of these social barriers that you find particularly challenging. Make a three-column chart. In the first column, indicate your assumption or stereotype. In the second column, note the source of your assumption. In the third column, after more reflection, note how you might work to overcome this attitude. If time allows, try this exercise with some of the other social barrier issues.

solidarity" (35).[4] If you are personally responsible for your own thoughts and behavior, participate by serving others with dignity and respect, and have worked to understand the underlying history and causes of inequity, then you will be transformed even as you seek to transform our society to more closely match the constitutional ideals of the equality and fair treatment of all.

## Privilege

In addition to stereotyping and assumptions, you will also need to deal with the concept of privilege. As a college student, you are perceived by others to be a privileged individual. In 2004 only 23.8 percent of the U.S. population had a college education; in other words, more than 75 percent of U.S. citizens have not completed the bachelor's degree that you seek (U.S. Census Bureau). Though you may think that you alone earned your place at college, all kinds of life conditions have contributed.

Peggy McIntosh, scholar and founder of the National S.E.E.D. Project on Inclusive Curriculum (Seeking Educational Equity and Diversity), is a nationally recognized authority on the subject of privilege.[5] She has developed numerous tools and has led workshops to examine privilege. She points out that "obliviousness of one's privileged state can make a person or group irritating to be with" and admits, "In my class and place, I did not see myself as a racist because I was taught to recognize racism only in individual acts of meanness by members of my group, never in invisible systems conferring unsought racial dominance on my group from birth." (2)

Take a moment to answer and contemplate your own experience in the light of the autobiographical list McIntosh developed, which she calls "an invisible

---

[4]Note that Kivisto uses the indefinite article *an* rather than *the*. He thus implies that we will not erase our other forms of chosen identity, such as ethnic or religious ties, but that citizenship as an identity that arches over our other identities will create commonality and a bridge where there had formerly been division and gulfs.

[5]McIntosh's work was first printed as Working Paper 189, "White Privilege and Male Privilege: A Personal Account of Coming to See Correspondences through Work in Women's Studies" (1988) at Wellesley College. It has since been widely disseminated and used in antiracism work. McIntosh is white and was considering her own privileges as a white woman by contrast with her African American colleagues in the same building and line of work."

# A Sample of Peggy McIntosh's Autobiographical List of White Privileges

1. I can, if I wish, arrange to be in the company of people of my race most of the time.

2. If I should need to move, I can be pretty sure of renting or purchasing housing in an area which I can afford and in which I would want to live. I can be pretty sure that my neighbors in such a location will be neutral or pleasant to me.

3. I can go shopping alone most of the time, pretty well assured that I will not be followed or harassed.

4. I can turn on the television or open to the front page of the paper and see people of my race widely represented.

5. When I am told about our national heritage or about "civilization," I am shown that people of my color made it what it is.

6. I can be sure that my children will be given curricular materials that testify to the existence of their race.

7. Whether I use checks, credit cards or cash, I can count on my skin color not to work against the appearance of financial reliability.

8. I can arrange to protect my children most of the time from people who might not like them.

9. I can swear, dress in second hand clothes or not answer letters, without having people attribute these choices to the bad morals, the poverty or the illiteracy of my race.

10. I can speak in public to a powerful male group without putting my race on trial.

11. I can do well in challenging situations without being called a credit to my race.

12. I am never asked to speak for all the people of my racial group.

13. I can be pretty sure that if I ask to talk to "the person in charge," I will be facing a person of my race.

14. I can go home from most meetings of organizations I belong to feeling somewhat tied in, rather than isolated, out-of-place, outnumbered, unheard, held at a distance or feared.

15. I can take a job with an affirmative action employer without having coworkers on the job suspect that I got it because of my race.

16. I can be sure that if I need legal or medical help, my race will not work against me.

17. I can easily buy posters, postcards, picture books, greeting cards, dolls, toys and children's magazines featuring people of my race.

18. I can remain oblivious of the language and customs of persons of color who constitute the world's majority without feeling in my culture any penalty for such oblivion.

19. If a traffic cop pulls me over or if the IRS audits my tax return, I can be sure I haven't been singled out because of my race.

20. If my day, week or year is going badly, I need not ask of each negative episode or situation whether it has racial overtones.

**Source:** From "White Privilege: Unpacking the Invisible Knapsack," *Peace and Freedom,* July/August 1989, pp. 10–12.

Activities which address immediate needs, but not always the conditions from which these needs emerge:
> Improving literacy skills of children, youth and adults through tutoring and teaching
> Serving food at a soup kitchen or shelter
> Answering calls for a suicide or sexual assault crisis hotline

Activities that identify and increase the human and/or economic assets of a neighborhood/community:
> Completing a neighborhood assets inventory
> Assisting with small business development or job skills development
> Offering leadership workshops to local residents
> Working to set up health care clinics and training community members on public health issues

Activities that mobilize people to influence public policy through formal political channels—campaign work, voting, voter registration:
> Organizing voter registration drives
> Working on a political campaign
> Creating or distributing candidates' profiles including records of support on various public issues

Activities that help make the world a little brighter for everyone:
> Biking, taking public transportation or carpooling to work or school
> Shopping at stores which give back to the communities they are located in directly
> Visit the www.thehungersite.com each day to order free food for the hungry
> Recycle paper, aluminum, glass, newspapers, plastic, etc.

Activities which raise awareness and/or change people's actions or attitudes about important social issues utilizing a range of educational approaches:
> Speaking to community groups about homelessness, crime and recycling in their local community
> Educating community groups through theater on AIDS/HIV prevention strategies or human rights issues
> Developing experimental workshops for groups to increase multicultural understanding

Activities that build trusting relationships among individuals and groups around issues of common concern:
> Participating in the national Million Man/Woman March
> Interviewing residents to document the history of a neighborhood
> Participating in emergency relief efforts after a flood, earthquake, tornado or hurricane
> Planting a community garden with other residents in your community as part of neighborhood revitalization efforts

Activities that identify allies, build common ground and implement strategies for changing public policy:
> Door-to-door campaigning for clean water action
> Lobbying for additional funding to build affordable housing
> Organizing a letter-writing campaign urging Congress to change existing welfare policy

Activities that use confrontation or public disobedience as a strategy for raising awareness of an issue or to change policy:
> Picketing or holding a candlelight vigil at the state capital
> Participating in Take Back the Night rallies and marches to protest sexual and domestic violence
> Organizing rallies to demand support for programs benefiting disadvantaged or underserved children

**FIGURE 3.1 Social Change Wheel: Models of Community Involvement**

Source: Adapted by Career & Community Learning Center, University of Minnesota, from a publication by Minnesota Campus Compact, 1996. © University of Minnesota.

weightless knapsack" full of the conferred privileges she experienced in her own particular place and work.

Once you are able to recognize instances of privilege, those you both do and do not have, you are better able to grasp the realities of social inequities. This realization can also help you move toward more openness to others, greater compassion, and a desire to change the system so that there is equity for all. Deciding to take action leads to service on the part of all in the community or, at the least, to the part of the community you are currently serving.

In essence, you must decide that you will be an ally to those you serve. An *ally* is *one who, though differing in makeup and background, willingly empathizes with the other and acts on behalf of the other*. Violence prevention expert and nationally acclaimed speaker and activist Paul Kivel urges, "We need to be thinking with others and noticing what is going on around us so we will know how to put our attention, energy, time and money toward strategic priorities in the struggle to end racism and other injustices" (127). If you are to be prepared for the future role you will play in society, service-learning will afford you a great learning opportunity to encounter, relate to, and work side by side as allies with many people who are different from you but share in citizenship of our world.

## The Social Change Wheel

This chapter on becoming good citizens is the theoretical foundation of why you should be engaged in the service-learning experience. In *Educating Citizens: Preparing America's Undergraduates for Lives of Moral and Civic Responsibility*, Ann Colby and her colleagues articulate a position that can serve as a summary of this chapter:

> If today's college graduates are to be positive forces in this world, they need not only to possess knowledge and intellectual capacities but also to see themselves as members of a community, as individuals with a responsibility to contribute to their communities. They must be willing to act for the common good and capable of doing so effectively. If a college education is to support the kind of learning graduates need to be involved and responsible citizens, its goals must go beyond mastery of a scholarly domain. They should include the competence to act in the world and the judgment to do so wisely. (7)

Service-learning will help you become a competent citizen who exercises informed public judgment in service and leadership. While relating and acting in community may not always be smooth sailing, the service-learning experience will give you a firsthand opportunity to improve your interpersonal skills, equipping you to function in the face of difference and conflict. In short, you will become a more productive and positive individual and community member, the kind of citizen our society needs.

As you reflect on becoming a productive citizen through service-learning, consider the Social Change Wheel developed by the Minnesota Campus Compact (Figure 3.1). The details of this wheel provide an excellent overview of how your service can contribute to our society even as you are learning and gaining new skills.

# 4 Preparing for Your Future

## Transferable Skills and Intentional Learning

Twenty-first century students are accustomed to quickly shifting trends, rapidly developing technology, and information overload from quick visuals and sound bites. By now, you probably already know that you must become adept at adaptation and must be a quick-change artist whose skills steady you to make necessary transitions over time. Will your education prepare you for flexibility and adaptation?

Historically, the United States has expected its colleges and universities "to prepare leaders, train employees, provide the creative base for scientific and artistic discovery, transmit past culture, create new knowledge, redress the legacies of discrimination, and ensure continuation of democratic principles" (Association of American Colleges and Universities iii). Today's colleges and universities face the additional challenges of sufficiently educating students for an increasingly complex, diverse, technology-based world. The AACU *Greater Expectations* report concludes that higher education must adapt to the challenges of the new millennium if it is to fulfill its role and responsibility.

This reality has caused colleges to focus curricular goals on helping you achieve "transferable intellectual capacities"[1] that you will need to move from one field of study or work to another:

> *Foundational skills* allow a person to do something; *intellectual capacities* enable a person to know when to do something, how to adapt it, and when to do it in a new way. Intellectual capacities not only provide the educated person with personal satisfaction, they also equip the self to deal constructively with the wider world. These capacities can increase career opportunities. They provide a person with the intellectual elasticity to confront the unexpected in personal and workplace life and to be productive participants in civic and cultural life. ("The Goals for Liberal Learning")

Such elasticity will prepare you for the many changes you will confront in life, including career changes, and will enable you to adapt, prosper, and contribute to your world in meaningful ways.

You can learn theories and study background information, practice foundational skills, analyze texts and problems, apply your knowledge in virtual situations, and participate in discussions to better your understanding in the classroom. However, you still may find yourself struggling to connect what you learn in one classroom to the content in another or to your daily life. Service-learning helps you make those connections and transferences. Sociologist Kathleen Weigert, director of the Center for Social Justice Research, Teaching and Service at Georgetown University, explains: "Because service-learning crosses so many boundaries, it offers new opportunities to think more consciously and more creatively about relationships, including those of faculty and student, disciplinary and interdisciplinary or multidisciplinary knowledge, campus and community" (7). When Weigert speaks of relationships, she goes beyond human connectedness and the faculty–student link. She acknowledges that service-learning helps you think about connections between courses and between the classroom and the wider world. As she indicates, service-learning helps you transfer learning in multiple ways that will positively affect your relationships, your knowledge, and your citizen role in community.

Because you must learn how to adapt to changing conditions and how to work with others, colleges and universities have increasingly adopted the service-learning approach that connects students with community partners and real needs. As consultants Toole and Toole explain, community service projects "involve complex problems, real-life contexts, and exposure to people who possess wide expertise and resources not found in school" (99). The best laboratories for applying learning are daily situations that challenge you to connect your learning to action, which is exactly the service-learning model. Rather

---

[1]This term is taken from "The Goals for Liberal Learning" at Concordia College-Moorhead, Minnesota, which were adopted January 16, 2004. Many other higher learning institutions have articulated similar goals and needs.

than a linear construct of learn first and then act, with service-learning you enter a never-ending cycle of learning: Your actions lead to learning, and you act on what you learn. This value-added type of education is gaining national recognition in both higher education and the corporate world.

Former Xerox CEO David T. Kearns describes the kind of education now necessary for today's competitive, global world of business:

> In such a world there is only one constant: change.... We need the flexible intellectual tools to be problem solvers, to be able to continue learning over time... [I]t is not simply what you know that counts, but the ability to use what you know. In this way, knowledge is power—the ability to use specialized knowledge as you adapt to new requirements. (qtd. in Association of American Colleges and Universities 28)

To create the kind of education Kearns insists is necessary today, the AACU report calls for "a dramatic reorganization of undergraduate education to ensure that all college aspirants receive not just access to college, but an education of lasting value" (vii).

What is "an education of lasting value"? What kind of learning do you need to achieve the flexible, practical, and adaptable kinds of knowledge and experience the twenty-first century world demands? You need educational experiences that go well beyond a list of books to read, assignments to finish, and courses to complete. Instead, the AACU *Greater Expectations* report asserts that higher education must provide educational experiences that create an intentional learner.

To become successful in the future, you must become an intentional learner now. As an *intentional learner*, you *set learning goals and shape experiences to attain those goals*. This attitude and behavior is strikingly different from treating learning as an incidental outcome of experiences.[2] Perhaps you are enrolled in a class that is required for your degree but that you wish you did not have to take. You attend class on a regular basis, take notes, and pass the tests, but you don't know why you have to take the course. You count on the instructor to make its relevance clear. If you learn anything, it will be almost incidental, a happy accident, because you do not have your own goals for learning. Whether the results of incidental learning last for long is questionable.

In contrast to an incidental learner, the intentional learner is self-directed and purposeful and understands the relationship between goals, the learning process, and appropriate action. Intentional learners understand how knowledge can be used in multiple ways for both the short term and the long term. They are "integrative thinkers who can see connections in seemingly disparate information and draw on a wide range of knowledge to make decisions. They adapt the skills learned in one situation to problems encountered in another: in a classroom, the workplace, their communities, or their personal lives." They recognize the connection between intellectual pursuits and their personal life and civic responsibilities. They also see themselves as part of a diverse world

---

[2]The term *intentional learner* was coined by Bereiter and Scardamalia, who contrast it with incidental learning.

**F**OCUS EXERCISE

**Acting as an Intentional Learner**

Think of a time other than a classroom experience when you really wanted to learn how to do something—play golf, set up your new computer software, or plan a trip, for example. What learning objectives did you set to achieve this goal? How successful were you? How much pleasure did you derive from your focused attempts at learning?

Now think of a time that you were excited about taking a class and knew exactly what you hoped to get out of it. What goals did you set for yourself in that class? What concrete steps did you take to achieve that goal? How did having such goals help you in your learning process? How much success or satisfaction did you derive from this classroom experience?

Consider how intentional goal setting and focused learning affect you. Set three goals for your current service-learning experience.

and are able to "draw on difference and commonality to produce a deeper experience of community" (Association of American Colleges and Universities 21–22). Service-learning, which integrates knowledge and community action, is designed to help you grow intellectually, personally, and civically. It helps you become the kind of intentional learner our world needs, preparing you for service and leadership in the world beyond college.

# Academic and Cognitive Abilities

Intentional learners are keen to develop specific academic and cognitive skills. Because the service-learning classroom is characterized by a high degree of integrative thinking and reflection, essential cognitive skills are taught, practiced, and reinforced through firsthand experiences. Some of the foundational skills enriched by the service-learning experience include reading, writing, listening, and speaking.

Course readings often directly connect to your service experience, and because the content has practical application, you build critical comprehension. Imran is a college junior, majoring in communications. For a communications theory course, he has been studying theories of groups, most recently reading about group norming. Imran and three classmates are participating in a service-learning project at a local assisted living center, where they must research, plan, and implement a weekly social activity for the residents. By reflecting on group dynamics as his small group performs the service task each week, Imran more clearly understands the group norming process he has been reading about in class. Service-learning often brings course content to life, and participants recognize the application of the material in everyday life, career choices, and lifelong learning.

Service-learning often provides multiple opportunities to process the service experience through written reflection and other course assignments. This allows you to further develop another crucial lifelong learning skill. A few years ago, for a special report on what employers look for in recent graduates, news anchor Peter Jennings visited with professionals on Wall Street, in Silicon Valley, and in Boston law firms. All the professionals with whom he spoke identified excellent writing skills as essential to success. Because service-learning often incorporates writing—from setting goals to reflecting on the experience and perhaps as service for your community partner—you will have many opportunities to refine this skill.

One student, Aron G., said this about how service-learning changed his writing skills for the better:

> In looking back over the service-learning journals, I noticed a couple main improvements. The first is my ability to think critically. In the beginning journals, I wasn't thinking "outside the box" very well; I was just focusing on the obvious. Now, as I review my latest journals, I have really stretched myself in "digging deeper" to address more abstract problems. The other major improvement that I have seen is in my writing ability. My fluency has increased quite a bit. Also, it seems as though my overall grammar skills have progressed. The improvement in these areas has most likely come from plain old practice. The more I write, as long as I put some time into it, the better it becomes.

Sophie G. and Jessica L. also indicated that service-learning improved their writing skills. According to Sophie G.:

> Service-learning helped me grow substantially as a writer. I really understand the importance of revision in my writing, and I now know that I can always keep moving it forward along the continuum. I think service-learning journals helped improve my writing because I was asked to write differently. We had to summarize and analyze, and knowing the difference and correct way to do each is substantial.

Jessica L. agreed: "I now feel that I can write more in depth. . . . I have learned to think critically about things and analyze them more to see past the surface."

These students are representative of many more who express the same sentiments. They indicate growth in elaboration of ideas, grammar skills, fluency, revision, summary, and analysis. They also recognize that their writing skills are directly connected to improved critical thinking.

Listening and speaking capacities often are also enhanced through service-learning. Interactions at the service site, discussions with fellow service-learning participants, and public presentations all help build critical listening and speaking skills. Casey, a predental student, helped a hospital chaplain plan weekly services for patients at the veterans hospital. In the process, he developed his speaking and presentation skills:

> This service-learning experience has helped me to grow my interpersonal skills far beyond my expectations. I have never thought of myself as being a good public speaker. . . . I remember the first time I gave the reading [in chapel], it was the busiest week with the most people. I stumbled with a lot of words and was deathly nervous. I gave my final reading last week and it went very well. I found that I was

a lot more comfortable being in front of a crowd and could speak more effectively. Now looking back at my interactions with the patients, I can see that now I am more likely to strike up a conversation than just standing there and smiling the entire time. I feel that this experience has helped me to become much more comfortable with public speaking as well as introducing myself and meeting new people. These new skills could prove to have profound implications on my later life. In giving presentations later in college, I will need to be comfortable speaking in front of a crowd. I want to one day become an orthodontist, and in order to do this successfully, I need to be comfortable starting up conversations with patients whom I barely know.

Casey is honest about his discomfort with speaking in front of others. Service-learning experiences are not always completely pleasant, but they provide the opportunity for growth. On reflection, Casey can appreciate that rising to meet the challenge resulted in improved listening and speaking skills. He also notes his personal growth and social skill development, topics addressed later in this chapter.

As the students noted, service-learning also expands critical thinking capabilities. *Critical thinking* is *a process that involves asking pertinent questions, weighing alternatives, evaluating evidence, forming arguments, and imagining possibilities*. As Walter, Knudsvig, and Smith summarize in *Critical Thinking: Building the Basics*, students who use critical thinking strategies "enhance their ability to focus, organize, categorize, process, and retrieve information. They think and learn information in more logical ways, which improves their ability to move up to higher levels of thinking" (vii). When you engage in critical thinking, you are doing more than seeking basic information; you are seeking understanding and wisdom that can be applied to daily life.

Another way to frame critical thinking comes from Gardner and Jewler. They describe four parts of critical thinking as abstract thinking, creative thinking, systematic thinking, and precise communication (30–31). During service-learning, you will exercise all four critical thinking functions. In a service-learning experience known as a Justice Journey during an alternative spring break, Midwestern students traveled to New Mexico to serve with and learn from Pueblo Indians. Objectives included learning about the history, culture, and contemporary issues of the Pueblo. The students cleared arroyos for water service, helped build a women's center, and assisted in the tribal school. They practiced abstract, creative, and systematic thinking as well as precise communication during the week of service-learning.

When students engaged in *abstract thinking*, they were *using details to discover a larger concept* (Gardner and Jewler 30). In the morning contemplation session before starting work on the women's center, students realized how little they knew about the role of women in the Pueblo culture. During an orientation session at the site, Kathy, the Pueblo manager of the project, provided background information and introduced the women who would be working alongside the students during construction. As the days progressed, students conversed with the locals, attended to habits and daily routines, observed relationships, and came to a greater understanding of challenges to and the importance of female leadership to the Pueblos. Through the details of their daily experiences, the students came to understand the larger, abstract concept of women's roles.

When participants engaged in *creative thinking*, they had to *seek connections, find new possibilities, and remain open to all ideas* (Gardner and Jewler 30). As students and community women discussed the possible uses of the center, they shared ideas about what they ideally envisioned and what could realistically be completed that week. All possibilities were openly considered. A number of needs and dreams were discussed, including how to create a space in which women could gather and talk about difficult issues in their lives. The women wanted a feeling of openness in this space. The group considered redesigning the living room or creating an intimate conversation room. They also

## FOCUS EXERCISE

### Developing as a Critical Thinker

In the lists below, circle the skills and traits that you possess, and underline those you need to work harder to develop.

### Skills of Critical Thinkers

1. Clarify concepts and beliefs
2. Recognize and formulate [anticipate potential] problems
3. Identify possible solutions
4. Gather relevant information
5. Be aware of assumptions, points of view, biases
6. Identify, formulate, and evaluate arguments
7. Weigh the merits of possible solutions
8. Evaluate possible solutions
9. Examine the consequences of accepting a solution

### Traits of Critical Thinkers

1. Analytic
2. Confident
3. Inquisitive
4. Persistent
5. Systematic
6. Tolerant
7. Truth seeking (Wall 43–44)

What is the difference between identifying, weighing, and evaluating solutions, and examining the consequences? Anticipate a problem that might call for problem-solving abilities during your service-learning experience. With a partner, identify, weigh, and evaluate possible solutions, and examine their consequences.

thought about constructing a screened-in porch that would be large enough to accommodate this kind of gathering. As the students and women brainstormed and dreamed together, a deeper connectedness and bond developed.

Eventually, they needed to move from broad, creative thinking to focusing on a solution. With *systematic thinking*, they *discarded the inessential and distracting and attended to organizing and prioritizing essential ideas and information that helped solve the problem* (Gardner and Jewler 31). The women and students dropped the idea of redesigning the living room or creating an intimate conversation room. They decided to build a screened-in porch because it most closely matched their dream of an open environment that would encourage conversation. Once this decision was made, they systematically went about drawing up the plans and gathering essential materials.

When students engaged in *precise communication* during the critical thinking process, they needed to *choose ways to effectively present ideas to others* (Gardner and Jewler 31). The students and the Pueblo women increasingly practiced precise communication as they worked together during the week. The students were expected to present their ideas during evening reflection sessions. Sometimes they were asked to describe what they were learning about the Pueblo culture and about themselves. On occasion during the morning contemplation session, individual students were given speaking assignments to prepare for that evening's group reflection. Both their daily communication and their presentation skills improved to make them more precise communicators.

As you consider all that the students were doing and learning during their Justice Journey experience, you can see that they were called on to practice critical thinking on a daily basis. In your own service-learning situation, you will need to ask questions, weigh alternatives, evaluate evidence, solve problems, analyze situations, and synthesize firsthand experience with other learning. As participants in service-learning, you will continually practice critical thinking during your work with your community partners while reflecting on what you are learning and applying that learning to your daily activities.

# Social and Interpersonal Skills

In addition to academic and cognitive skills, participants often experience personal and social growth as a result of service-learning. Eyler, Giles, and Gray list dozens of studies that document personal and social outcomes of service-learning (19–20). Learning to successfully navigate new social situations results in growth in confidence, cooperative ability, self-awareness, and compassion.

Service-learning situations provide opportunities to practice the social and interpersonal skills that are expected of competent adults in the workplace. The directors of Be Globally Focused, an international consulting firm for higher education and business, provide a concise description of these skills:

> Interpersonal communication is the process of interacting with people to maximize the presence of the personal. It is a personal quality of contact that goes beyond a social exchange and includes active listening, the validation of nonverbal

cues, and the recognition of the uniqueness of the other person. Communicating effectively interpersonally means understanding the dynamics of the interpersonal exchange and being actively involved in the co-creation of shared meaning between two or more people in the work place. (Ellingboe)

The terms *social* and *interpersonal* indicate that at least two people are involved in the communication process. Communication calls for an open style in which you both give and receive. For example, Aron found it necessary to develop his interpersonal and social skills in order to effectively relate to his Adopt-a-Grandparent partner, whose ability to speak clearly was impaired by a stroke:

> I definitely believe that my interpersonal skills were stretched during my time with Bob. The most stretching happened during the first few days with Bob and probably the last day when I left. The first day was especially difficult because I was introduced to a complete stranger. What made it even harder was that Bob was super difficult to understand. I had to try and create conversations, and at the same time try and piece together the words Bob was saying. The last day will also be difficult because I have developed a strong relationship and it will be hard to find an easy way to say goodbye. Developing my interpersonal skills will surely help me in my future in interviews, meeting new people, and developing more meaningful relationships.

Aron understood that working with Bob was both a challenge and an opportunity. Over the course of the semester, he and Bob built a relationship by finding a way to communicate and connect. Aron also appreciated that the

**FOCUS EXERCISE**

**Developing Social and Interpersonal Competence and Confidence**

Think of a time you experienced a new social situation. For example, recall your first days in college or on a new job. What challenges to your social and interpersonal skills did you encounter? How did you meet those challenges? What kinds of social and interpersonal challenges, if any, do you anticipate at your service site? What kinds of social and interpersonal skills are necessary for success in your personal and professional life after college?

interpersonal and social skills he developed would translate to future situations. As you practice your interpersonal and social skills, you will develop competencies that will help you now and in the future.

Through the service experience you may be exposed to people from a wide range of backgrounds and life experiences, which can make you more confident about your ability to adjust to diverse social encounters. Kristen, a nursing student, provided social companionship to an elderly woman at the site where Aron served. Kristen had little experience with the elderly, and she expressed nervousness about the social situation at the beginning of her service-learning experience: "I'm just not sure what to say or do with Helen. She can't see very well, and she seems so fragile. I want to say and do the right things when I'm with her, but she only answers 'yes' or 'no' when I ask her questions."

After several weekly visits, Kristen reflected on her increased confidence:

> I think I've been protecting myself for a long time by not making myself take on new challenges like the Adopt-a-Grandparent program. I've always had a hard time being open with people, but I can now see how that has been affecting my relationships with others. My weekly visits with Helen have become something I look forward to. I've learned how to ask the right kinds of questions so I get more than "yes" or "no" responses from her. Sometimes we laugh together and share things about our day-to-day lives, which we didn't do at the beginning. I know I am going to miss Helen when this class ends because she has taught me a lot about myself and about older people.

Kristen's journal is indicative of increased social confidence in new and challenging situations. Because of her participation in service-learning, her social skills have been enhanced, and her life and the lives of those she touches have been enriched.

You also may gain confidence when you see that your service has made a significant difference. This sense of *efficacy—the ability to effect change—* will benefit you as you respond to life's challenges in the future. In *Where's the Learning in Service-Learning?* Eyler and Giles address the way service-learning provides a sense of efficacy: "Beyond seeing real events and situations and knowing people affected by community issues, students also often had genuine work to do and found this work strongly motivating. One of the differences between rich simulated exercises and service-learning is that students know that the work they are doing makes a difference in someone's life besides their own" (89).

In *When Hope and Fear Collide: A Portrait of Today's College Students*, Arthur Levine and Jeanette S. Cureton also underscore the necessity of an undergraduate education that provides students with opportunities to develop efficacy, the "sense that one can make a difference." Levine and Cureton remind students of their potential effect on others: "Today's students need to believe that they can make a difference. Not every one of them will become president of the United States, but each of them will touch scores of lives far more directly and tangibly—family, friends, neighbors, and coworkers. For ill or for good, in each of those lives students will make a difference" (159–160).

Jessica, a math tutor, reflected that "The most meaningful day for me was when I watched my work make a difference. I was teaching a young girl how to do her math. After she had completed half of the paper, she was breezing by everything. There is nothing to describe how good you feel after you see results of your work." This sense of efficacy is critical, especially for today's college students.

As you become more socially confident, service-learning increases your ability to work with others. Through service experiences, you learn to work cooperatively. Both at the service site and in the classroom, you engage in shared decision making and problem solving, you exchange personal stories, and you participate in group discussion and interaction. Your group skills are expanded because you must work collaboratively to integrate service experiences with learning objectives. Group or teamwork skills also develop through group projects and presentations in which you must communicate effectively with your group and the audience.

Bruce Litchfield, a professor of agricultural engineering who uses service-learning, begins his Learning in Community (LINC) course with a demonstration of teamwork. He asks eight students to come to the front of the room and toss a tennis ball around the group, including each member in the exercise. As they proceed, he tosses in more balls of different types and even a rubber duck. To make the game more challenging, he places a chair in the middle of the group. By this time, the rest of the students are laughing uproariously. Then the professor brings the class back to the learning moment with a discussion of how teamwork had to be implemented. He uses this demonstration to introduce students to the need for teamwork in their semester-long service-learning projects: "Lessons learned: Teamwork requires focus, communication, organization, practice, adjusting to personalities. It also requires the ability to deal with unclear goals and unforeseen obstacles, like the chair." He makes the connection between the activity and service-learning, pointing out that the teamwork task is filled with ambiguity and complexity, just as the service-learning experience may be:

> [S]tudents would not be given a specific problem to solve. They would have to work out for themselves, in consultation with the client, what their project would be for the semester, the scope of it, and how they would accomplish it. They would also have to learn how to work as a team, dealing with communication issues, personality conflicts, and budget and time constraints. At the end, they would have to

accept there would be no right or wrong answer, no "nice round number when you're done," said Ann Finnegan, LINC's program manager. In other words, it's a lot like projects in the real world, said Litchfield, a professor of agricultural engineering and the director of LINC. "It's messy, and we expect it to be messy." (Chamberlain)

As with any situation that involves multiple people, unforeseen challenges may arise during your service-learning experience. But if you implement the lessons of teamwork, you and the people with whom you work can keep the proverbial ball in the air. You will adapt when and how you need to adapt, and you will learn to work together.

In addition to working well in groups, service-learning can also deepen your self-understanding and show you why you think and behave the way you do. Because Casey, who worked with the veterans hospital chaplain, enjoyed his service experience so much, he decided to invite his roommate, Alex, to help:

> I'm glad I invited Alex to come along. When I first thought about inviting him, I decided against it. I now realize this was because I had found a good thing, and I didn't want to share it with anyone else. I remembered what I learned in another course, however, what Socrates said about friendship. He said that a good friend will share his good experiences so his friend can also have the same joys. My service experience has taught me about what it takes to be a good friend.

Casey has gained deeper self-awareness and an improved perception of the nature of his relationships with others. Because of his experience, he will be a better friend and better equipped to work well with others. He will not just think about himself but will consider the gifts and needs of those around him.

**FOCUS EXERCISE**

**Practicing Compassionate Connectedness**

Were you ever in the position of sympathizer, and did you, on reflection, feel superior to the person with whom you were sympathizing? Were you ever the recipient of someone else's sympathy, and did you feel inferior to that person? If you cannot think of a personal example, have you ever witnessed an exchange of sympathy that created a negative hierarchy?

Think about Watson's statement, and contemplate its meaning for you and your service situation. What can you do to ensure that you practice the positive power of compassionate connectedness rather than the disempowering attitude of sympathy? Write down three reminders that will help shape your attitude and action.

Because you are continually relating to and with others in service-learning, the experience provides the opportunity to develop *compassion. Compassion* involves *connectedness, the notion of being and walking with a person;* it is not the same as offering sympathy, which creates a hierarchy in which the sympathizer is dominant. In fact, some service-learning participants who sympathize may be tempted to take control because they believe that they understand and know best what others need. People who practice compassionate connectedness do not attempt to control others. Rather, they respect the capacity of others and the ability of people to understand their own lives. They see that other people can participate in working toward solutions and can lead those offering service toward greater understanding of their own lives as well as the lives of the people they are serving.

Lilla Watson, an Australian aboriginal activist, cautioned those who were working with her community in an effort to end poverty: "If you have come here to help me, you are wasting your time. . . . But if you have come because your liberation is bound up with mine, then let us work together" (qtd. in Bricker-Jenkins et al). Watson was eager to collaborate with those who would walk alongside, but she insisted that the attitude must be mutual respect and shared responsibility. Keeping her caution in mind can help you practice compassionate connectedness.

# Finding Your Calling

Whether you are on a path toward a specific career or you have not yet decided on a major or profession, service-learning may help you find your calling or vocation. Though the terms *calling* and *vocation* once invoked religious professions such as priesthood, today they mean *employing your particular talents and gifts in community with others as a way of living your lifework.* Contemporary theologian Frederick Buechner underscores the place of vocation in the lives of all working people: Vocation is more than just a job; it is "the place where your deep gladness and the world's deep hunger meet" (118–119).

Clinical psychologist John Neafsey has expanded Buechner's concept into a course called Personal Vocation and Social Conscience. Neafsey points out that "Vocation is not only about 'me' and my personal fulfillment, but about 'us' and the common good. . . . Authentic vocational discernment, therefore, seeks a proper balance between inward listening *to* our hearts and outward, socially engaged listening *with* our hearts to the realities of the world in which we live" (1). It makes sense that vocation is always also about the communities in which we live and work. As discussed in Chapter 3, none of us lives in isolation; the individual is shaped by and consists of others in our lives. Therefore, you can discover your vocation only by attending to your inner desires and to the world's needs.

Striking the kind of balance encouraged by Buechner and Neafsey presents a challenge that may seem overwhelming. Exploring your calling or vocation, especially the first time, may raise anxieties and questions: What am I supposed to do with my life? What is my "deep gladness"; what truly gives me joy and a sense of deep satisfaction? How can what makes me joyful meet one of the "world's deep hunger[s]," that is, a real need? How will my work serve the wider community? How should I earn my living, and what is the connection of my occupation to my calling? What's the best way for me to accomplish my life and career goals while engaging with others in my world?

Most often, vocation is not something you define once and for all. Instead, your calling can serve as an anchor throughout your lifetime as you redefine and revise your career in response to changes within yourself and in the world around you.

On graduation, having focused her studies in communications, Becky worked as a successful sales representative for a major pharmaceutical company. This first job made use of her communication skills and furthered an interest in medicine developed during a hospital internship focused on corporate communication. She met directly with doctors to promote drugs manufactured by her company. Becky began to feel that her greatest gifts were not being used on behalf of others. Because the managers of the pharmaceutical company valued Becky's communication skills and personable manner, they worked to find a more suitable way for her talents to serve the corporation. During the past few years, Becky has worked at corporate headquarters training the sales force. In this capacity, she helps others develop their communication and teamwork skills. This career is a much better fit for Becky and the company.

Becky is also looking ahead. Every month she saves a portion of her salary to prepare to respond even more strongly to her calling. Becky dreams of starting and serving as managing director of a theatre. When she fulfills her dream—and it is only a matter of time—she will use her communication expertise and her business sense to bring a richer arts experience to her community. Becky has recognized that her calling—her deepest joy and satisfaction—comes from working closely with others in team situations, whether in business or the arts. Despite many turns in her career journey, that single calling anchors her life.

Though many people change careers, and many even sense new callings at some point, learning how to discern the best way for you to work in the world is deeply gratifying and focuses your life. Whether you sense one calling or many, living out your vocation is a lifelong journey. To live a life of calling, you must look for opportunities to develop transferable career and life skills, explore diverse communities in new ways, practice interaction with a wide range of individuals, connect learning with action, and reflect on new understandings with broad applications.

Service-learning is one process that can help you practice important life skills to help you discern vocation and successfully live your calling throughout your lifetime. Kara's service-learning experience helped her explore her sense of calling:

> Service-learning has helped to influence my understanding of vocation. When I first came to college, I was on the pre-med track with a double major in biology and chemistry. . . . Serving at Eventide [Nursing Home] has helped me to see [that] . . . if I were to become a doctor, I honestly do not think I could be a geriatrics specialist. I do enjoy working with the elderly, but at times I think I might get depressed dealing with illness affecting the elderly. I would prefer family practice or something close to that concerning a wide variety of ages. . . . After serving at Eventide, I also have realized that doctors establish relationships, but may only see that patient every five months or so. I would want to see them get better and be there through the healing process. . . . Having an actual understanding of the patient–doctor relationship has prompted me to lean more strongly toward an English major and the possibility of teaching. Many options remain available for my future, but this first-hand experience has been beneficial to my overall decision.

The service-learning partnership helped Kara explore her interests and strengths so she could more carefully choose a major and vocation that suits her. The service experience enabled her to envision herself in different career situations, helping her explore the place where her "deep gladness" (establishing relationships) might indeed meet "the world's deep hunger" (educating others).

Numerous resources indicate the same general steps for finding a fulfilling and effective calling. For instance, both the Career Center at Berkeley and the professional business organization CoachVille emphasize the need for experience, specifically suggesting experimenting through volunteering. The CoachVille website emphatically states that "There's no substitute for experience, the more the better. . . . And don't rely on a single authority or work experience" (Paul 2). Berkeley Career Center advises, "Through direct experience, you gain the kind of exposure that can best educate you about yourself and your compatibility with different jobs or careers" (2). The exposure and experience that service-learning provides will help you discover a great deal about yourself and about what you want to do with your life.

Perhaps you have already been drawn to a path in life, and you hope for a service-learning experience that will allow you to meet the needs of others while also helping you learn and gain experience in your field of study. As executive career coach Shale Paul states, "Within the bounds of the area you've picked, try to get as much and as varied experience as you can. If you're committed to finding out about a certain career, you may want to consider volunteering in order to gain experience. That way, you'll be able to test out whether it fits your values and preferences. If you aren't getting paid to do it, chances are you won't stay with it unless you like it" (2).

Wouldn't it be wonderful to discover that you like a particular kind of work well enough to do it because it suits you rather than because you get paid? Through service-learning, you may discover the work that gives you joy. Service-learning becomes so much more valuable when you recognize that you are learning not only about course objectives but also about yourself and your life skills, that it can serve as the entry to your calling into career and into the rest of your life. First you must be willing to make the most of the opportunity and to focus on serving and learning.

Imagine that your professor has arranged to connect the class with a daycare center for children from low-income families. At first glance, you see a daycare as a match only for students of early childhood education or social work. However, the needs of this agency may call for skills other than teaching and tending children. Perhaps you are an architecture or engineering student, and daycare center staff bemoan the shortage of space for all the center's needs. You learn that the center has no extra funding for expansion. You begin to take stock of how space is allotted and consider how it might be reconfigured for better use. You ask the director whether you could help by drawing up a new set of plans and supervising a relatively cost-free reconfiguration of the center.

Or perhaps you are an accounting or economics major. Most staff members at the daycare center come from the education and social service sectors, but someone is needed to keep the place financially viable. Is there a need for help with the center's accounting or budgeting. Perhaps there are several budgets. Could the accounts be simplified and unified? Maybe there is one budget that needs clearer specification and separate accounts. Perhaps a fellow student in computer programming could set up a program to track accounts, saving the cost of expensive accounting software.

The list of needs and connections to courses and student abilities is virtually endless. The important points are that service is done on the part of real need and that in the process you learn invaluable lessons. Or course, not all the lessons are discipline-specific, nor need they be.

## ●F OCUS EXERCISE

### Taking Stock of Your Own Abilities and Gifts

Individually or working with a partner who knows you well, make a list of the abilities that others have recognized in you. Consider how these abilities could be an asset to your community partner. Now make a list of areas in which you think you need growth, whether in skills, intellectual capacities, or character traits. If you already have a service site selected, write one paragraph about how you might use your particular abilities at this site, and write a second paragraph about how serving at this site might help you grow in needed areas.

# Career Understanding, Work Preparedness, and Equipped for the Future (EFF) Skills

Statisticians tell us that people who are just entering the working world can expect to change jobs as many as eight times by the time they are thirty-two and up to twenty times over the course of their lives.[3] Knowing and honing your abilities and gifts will help you focus as you enter the working world.

When college graduates apply for positions, employers look at more than transcripts and student GPAs. In *10 Things Employers Want You to Learn in College*, Bill Coplin points out that employers also want an idea of your "*Know-How Score*," *your abilities gained from experiences beyond the classroom setting.* According to Coplin, three aspects make service-learning particularly relevant. First, employers like students to have actual work experience in addition to coursework. Service-learning sites can provide experience that will make you more competitive in the job market. Second, employers value workers who know how to cooperate well with and for others:

> Doing good without a credit or monetary payoff is viewed by many employers as valuable for another reason. Such work can mean that you are the type of person who can work for something bigger than yourself. The step from good citizen in the volunteer sector to a team player within the business world is small. (Coplin 191)

Third, employers want to see focus—sustained service rather than "a lot of scattered activities" (191), which is exactly where service-learning excels. While volunteering may happen in short bursts, service-learning calls for an extended commitment across time.

Think carefully about the three aspects of experience that employers have identified and how service-learning can help you grow in these areas. Now turn to the Focus Exercise and determine your own Know-How Score.[4]

Most of us can improve our Know-How Scores. Service-learning provides opportunities to do so, better preparing you for your future workplaces.

Today's employers seek worker-leaders who are ready for the challenges of a complex, ever-changing work environment. Are these the kind of workers entering the job force today? In an article in *The Chronicle of Higher Education*, Mel Levine says no: "We are witnessing a pandemic of what I call 'worklife unreadiness,' and colleges face a daunting challenge in immunizing students against it." He contends that "many contemporary college and graduate students fail to identify at all with the world of adults," leading to "an unsuccessful crossover from higher education to the workplace." Employers desire employees who can effectively organize and manage time and materials, prioritize, integrate, apply

---

[3] This statistic can be found in numerous sources, including on page 4 of Taylor and on page xi of Enelow and Kursmark.

[4] Although Coplin provided the concept and term *Know-How Score*, he did not provide a formula for actually determining a score. Based on his concept, we have developed a process to help you arrive at an actual score.

## FOCUS EXERCISE

### Determining Your Know-How Score

Draw three columns and title them *practical experience, cooperative experience,* and *service experience.* In the first column, list the beyond-classroom experiences that you bring to the world of work, such as trips you've made or jobs you've held. In the second column, describe situations that have called for your coopera-tion with others, such as completing a group project or participating in team sports. What did you learn from these experiences, and how can you translate that learning to future work situations? In the third column, if you have partici-pated in sustained service, describe the kind of service and what you learned from the experience.

Next, exchange your answers with a partner. Each of you should score the three categories of experience on the following scale:

1 = Little experience

2 = Moderate experience

3 = Extensive experience

Now total the three scores to get an overall Know-How Score. Discuss the scores and how you arrived at your evaluation. The overall scores can be valued as follows:

0–3 = Needs much more experience that will transfer to the working world

4–7 = Needs to continue seeking active experiences as learning opportunities

8–9 = Seems well-prepared for the working world; should accept and practice leadership roles

learning, collaborate, problem solve, and communicate effectively in multiple ways. This is a tall order for many graduates entering today's job market: "cur-rent students face complex decision-making and problem-solving career chal-lenges, but many have been groomed in high school to rely solely on rote memory—an entirely useless approach in a meaningful career" (Levine B11).

Service-learning does not rely on rote memory; rather, it challenges you to learn through experience and application. Students involved in service-learning not only gain job-related skills, but they also sometimes use the service experience to demonstrate their interests and abilities to future employers. For example, a stu-dent who wrote grant applications with a community partner may demonstrate interest and skill in grant writing.

Service-learning is one of the keys to having the know-how for success in both work and life. Coplin urges students to select a college based on the opportunity to participate in service-learning:

> You want to go to a school that encourages and supports public- and community-service activities. . . . Check with students and determine whether or not the col-lege or university is a member of Campus Compact, an organization that was established to promote community-based learning throughout the United States. Institutions that are members are more likely to take service-learning seriously than those that are not members. (134)

Since you are reading this text, your college probably takes service-learning seriously, recognizing how important it is to your learning and preparation as well as how necessary it is to the wider community.

Students often develop practical skills necessary for future careers—such as punctuality, responsibility, and time management—through service-learning. In some cases, service-learning provides opportunities for participants to explore possible career choices. In addition to helping you practice career skills, community-based service-learning may also introduce you to professionals and other volunteers who model passion for and competency in their work. In short, you will understand and appreciate more clearly what is demanded in the world of work.

As a prepharmacy major, Neil participated in service-learning at a local hospital pharmacy. Because his father is a small-town pharmacist, he thought he "knew what it would be like." But "I was wrong. It was so much more. This pharmacy had mechanical prescription equipment and many pharmacists." Neil describes his service and interaction with the pharmacy professionals:

> My main job was to help the techs. These jobs were usually filling kits for pre-appointments, like enemas to prepare for colonoscopies. In addition I made simple lotions and ointments. I also cleaned and threw away expired drugs. One thing that I did not think would happen was that I would create a connection with some of the employees there. As I started to work with the techs and pharmacists, I learned a lot about them and their lives. The connection was amazing.

Neil learned more than he expected about his future career, and he also had the wonderful opportunity to see that career modeled by several caring professionals.

To make sure that you are prepared for a productive future, you should become familiar with employer expectations at basic entry-level jobs. The Equipped for the Future (EFF) Standards developed by the National Institute for Literacy "define the knowledge and skills adults need in order to successfully carry out their roles as parents, citizens, and workers in the 21st Century."[5] The sixteen standards are grouped into four categories: Communication Skills, Interpersonal Skills, Decision-Making Skills, and Lifelong Learning Skills (see Figure 4.1).

Communicating effectively calls for you to speak, listen, read, write, and observe in ways that create a growth of understanding. Interpersonal skills require you to act cooperatively, negotiate appropriately, and resolve conflict effectively. Other interpersonal skills that EFF stresses include guiding others and acting as an advocate for others. Decision-making skills go hand-in-hand with problem solving. Being a lifelong learner includes the abilities to research and to take responsibility for your own learning, the kind of proactive behavior we have called "intentional learning."

Take time to work with the EFF Standards by completing the Focus Exercise.

---

[5]See <http://www.nifl.gov/nifl/eff.html> for information on this movement, which will also direct you to a more extensive discussion of EFF at the University of Tennessee-Knoxville <http://eff.cls.utk.edu/fundamentals/default.htm>.

**FIGURE 4.1    The Sixteen EFF Content Standards**

---

**ⅎOCUS EXERCISE**

**Developing EFF Standards**

After studying Figure 4.1, think about how the standards apply to your course-work. Which ones do your current courses emphasize? Which do you think you need the most help developing? How might working with your community partner help you achieve these standards?

---

The service-learning site and the people with whom you work become your greatest resource for learning, resulting in an active research process through which you fulfill learning objectives and achieve skills standards. As you consider the EFF standards and reflect on this chapter, note that the professionals, from the academics to the CEOs, agree on the essentials. In short, service-learning prepares you to enter the world of work with the skills necessary to succeed.

*Online Study Center* college.hmco.com/PIC/duncan1e

# How Does Service-Learning Work?

# Participating in an Integrated Experience

## Roles of Service-Learning Participants: Campus Facilitators, Community Partners, and Students

**LEARNING OBJECTIVES**

After studying this chapter and doing the exercises, you should be able to

- Describe the roles of the key individuals involved in your service experience
- Identify the difference between a learning goal, an objective, and an outcome
- Identify several methods of assessment that are useful in service-learning
- Complete organizational tasks essential to success in service-learning
- Assess your own preparedness for success in service-learning

The service-learning method of teaching and learning changes the way we view the traditional classroom learning context. In the traditional classroom, two roles are predominant: the teacher role and the student role. Historically, their realm of interaction has been the hallowed halls of academia, where the privileged few engage in higher learning. The notion of a separate realm has led some to refer to the relationship between the wider community and higher education as "town and gown." The term implies that the two realms have no connection and no intersection. It has led to the old notion that the academy is not part of the real world and that only when college students finish their education do they join the real world.

However, the notion of the ivory-tower gowned realm versus the practical everyday world never was accurate and is completely dispelled by the service-learning movement. Service-learning pedagogy places you in intersecting realms, expanding and redefining the roles of those who participate in the teaching and

91

learning process. The nature of the educational experience is transformed when service is incorporated to achieve established learning goals and address genuine community issues. Whereas the traditional classroom setting most often focuses on the role and relationship between teacher and student, service-learning usually adds additional key people to the learning equation.

It is important to understand some of the responsibilities of people who might be part of your service-learning experience because you will be in a shared relationship with them. No two service-learning situations are identical, and not all of the roles described will apply to your situation.

## Campus Facilitators

Campus facilitators may include faculty members, a service-learning director and staff members, student affairs personnel, and campus organizations. Faculty members are central to service-learning because they often make the decision to implement this learning method in the classroom. Instructors create the course syllabus that articulates the course objectives and describes the service-learning philosophy, its relationship to the course, and its relationship to the concept of engaged citizenship (see Chapter 3).

The faculty role often includes communicating with the community partners, with other campus personnel connected with the service project, and with student participants. Members of any or all of these groups may participate in designing the course syllabus. Faculty members also structure and facilitate opportunities for critical reflection to ensure that the service is meaningfully connected to the learning objectives.

Faculty members monitor participation in the service project, offering guidance and assistance as necessary. In some instances, staff members of a campus service-learning office assist with such oversight. Finally, because service-learning likely partially determines students' overall course grades, the instructor sets up a process for evaluation, consulting with the community partner when possible.

Not all higher education institutions have designated a service-learning director or office. However, many colleges and universities do have a service-learning director, a service-learning coordinator, or a director of experiential learning. This individual may have a small staff or may be part of a larger institutional center, such as a community service or civic leadership center.

The service-learning director is responsible for providing resources about service-learning pedagogy, for connecting community agencies and faculty members, for facilitating the partnership process, for coordinating off-campus service experiences, and for assisting faculty members and participants as necessary throughout the service cycle. This role may also involve seeking additional funding for campus service-learning efforts and completing institutional paperwork and reports about service-learning efforts on campus. In addition, directors often work with budgets that relate to service-learning on campus. The service-learning director or office may be a part of the division of academic affairs or the division of student affairs.

Student affairs personnel are concerned with the social, emotional, physical, and mental well-being of students as they live, study, work, and interact with each other in the academic environment. At a growing number of colleges and universities, designated student affairs personnel facilitate opportunities for service-learning as part of students' intellectual and social engagement with the institution and the broader community. They may also determine objectives, set procedures, guide reflection, and carry out evaluation. Often the service-learning office and campus organizations are a part of the larger student affairs division, which oversees their practices and policies and partners with them in the overall life and learning of students.

Sometimes campus groups or organizations such as fraternities, athletic teams, and residence halls incorporate service-learning to help achieve specific objectives. A campus organization using this method of learning is responsible for complying with college policies, expectations, and structures to ensure quality service-learning experiences.

## Community Partners

Often a site supervisor at the community agency coordinates and directs the service at the particular site. In quality service-learning, the site supervisor is an essential partner in a meaningful college–community relationship. The site supervisor often plays a critical role in determining and communicating the genuine needs and assets of the agency and those served, and then helps plan the service-learning experience so that the work is valuable to the agency and to the participants.

The responsibilities of the site supervisor often include providing on-site orientation such as general history, mission, and goals of the agency; describing day-to-day workings of the agency; communicating information about those served by the agency; informing student participants about their responsibilities; offering necessary training to student participants; and serving as a contact for the college institution and the service site. Some site supervisors also coordinate participants' service placements and schedule suitable service times. In some instances, the site supervisor might complete documentation or evaluation of students' service work, such as by compiling records of the number of hours served.

The service agency may have paid staff members who carry out some of the daily work. These people help fulfill the mission, goals, and daily commitments of the agency. Through the important work of the agency staff, service-learning participants may gain valuable knowledge about issues related to the focus of the service and study.

Sometimes there are volunteers at a service site. Volunteers freely give of their time to provide service or assistance without compensation. They may individually decide to give of their time and abilities, or they may be part of a group or organization. Often, they work closely with service-learning students, though they are not focused on learning objectives or the reciprocal relationship of service-learning.

Unlike the other roles, which have designated and specific functions, the people known as clients participate in or benefit from the community agencies in some way. They are living complicated lives that intersect with others

**F**OCUS EXERCISE

**Considering Roles and Responsibilities**

Identify the people who play the various roles in the coordination of your service-learning experience. Do they go by titles other than those identified in this chapter, or are they part of divisions or categories not discussed? Write a brief contemplation on how you will be expected to interact with them.

After you have interacted with the respective parties, reread your contemplation. How did the interaction mirror your expectations? How might you alter your descriptions? How can any of these individuals enhance your experience, especially if or when you encounter difficulties?

in their respective roles. The *clients*, that is, *the individuals or groups served by various community agencies*, play a critical role, though sometimes indirectly, in teaching service-learning students about the agency, the community, themselves, and the world around them.

Be observant at your service site and follow the lead of the agency in referring to those served. Also be mindful of your language in class discussion so that you dignify these individuals.

## Student Participants

In most situations, your service site has been selected and much of the service-learning experience has been planned for you. Occasionally, you may have the responsibility of choosing a service site, contacting the agency to determine what work is necessary, and scheduling suitable work times. Although your role as student-participant will vary from one service-learning context to the next, you must assume two roles: service provider and learner. You are responsible for attending site orientation and training sessions, contemplating carefully as you prepare for service, carrying out the actions that are expected of you, and critically reflecting on the experience, striving to connect your actions with the desired learning goals. You should also participate to the best of your ability and communicate clearly with others involved in the service relationship, such as the campus facilitator, the site supervisor, the agency staff, and those served.

# Identifying Learning Objectives and Outcomes

As you begin your service-learning experience, you need to clearly understand the desired learning outcomes and why certain forms of assessment are implemented. Understanding the objectives and outcomes of a course also may help you understand why you must fulfill certain requirements that constitute part of your grade. As Aristotle told his son Nicomachus, you cannot hit the target if you do not know what the target is. While goals indicate in broad terms what you and/or your campus facilitator hope you will achieve, objectives define more specific behavior needed to achieve the overall goals. Outcomes indicate what has been achieved that can be measured by assessment instruments.

Consider another sports analogy. In a football game, the overall goal is to score more points than the opposition by getting the ball into the end zone to win the game. Each team must achieve objectives along the way: to keep the ball and move it toward their goal. Measuring whether the ball has been moved far enough on each play assesses whether each objective has been met. The outcome of meeting an objective is that the ball has been moved far enough to let the team retain possession. Applied to service-learning, the *goal* is *what you want to achieve by the end of the experience. Objectives* are the *steps along the way that enable you to achieve a goal. Outcomes* are *the result of your learning that can be readily measured, or assessed.*

Assessment is an integral part of education and is used to determine whether you are actually learning. To some extent, what will be assessed guides what will be taught and what you are expected to do. Take a look at the Aligning the Learning Experience box. This example spells out the way the entire learning experience is aligned, from setting goals to selecting a teaching method to measuring what the student has actually learned.

## Aligning the Learning Experience

**Goal:** Development of empathy

**Objectives to Achieve the Goal:**
By the end of the service experience, the student will be able to

- Describe the attributes of the community partner

- Write a story that narrates a day in the life of the community partner

- Make an argument for additional support from the wider community to the partner

**Type of Assessment:** Interview, journal entry or story, and essay

**Outcome:** The student will be able to see that she or he has developed empathy.

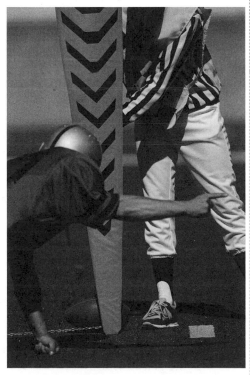

Often it is difficult to assess all that has been learned, especially when the pedagogy is based on actual experience and personal transformation. Chapter 4 addresses the kinds of foundational skills and transferable capacities you will develop as well as the ways in which your critical thinking abilities will expand. In addition to these types of skills, other outcomes are often overlooked. In "Assessing Community Service-Learning: Are We Identifying the Right Outcomes?" Adrianna Kezar notes: "First, the current assessment methods do not adequately capture students' complex development. Second, these methods often assess a narrow set of outcomes, leaning heavily toward traditional cognitive outcomes such as critical thinking and GPA" (15).

To identify meaningful outcomes and truly measure what you can gain from service-learning, consider carefully what you can expect as results of service-learning:

> [I]nvolvement in service-learning was most highly correlated with tolerance and breaking down stereotypes, interpersonal development (working with others, leadership, communication skills), personal development (self-knowledge, spiritual growth, finding reward in helping others), and linkages between community and college (making connections to community, developing friendships). The next most significant outcome was increased citizenship skills, including values, knowledge, skills, efficacy, and commitment to social responsibility. (Eyler and Giles, in Kezar 16)

All these skills are critical to living a successful and purposeful life.

Perhaps because of such significant development, students themselves report that they value their service-learning experience highly. In a study of college graduates, Peter Dillon and Robyn Van Riper reported that those who had been involved in service-learning considered it "among their most valuable learning experiences" and one that made them "more likely to assume leadership positions" (qtd. in Kezar 16).

## Possible Service-Learning Outcomes

By the end of the service-learning experience, you will

- Make connections to community
- Develop traits of an engaged citizen
- Break down stereotypes
- Increase tolerance
- Work collaboratively with others
- Find satisfaction in helping others
- Develop friendships
- Enhance communication skills
- Grow spiritually
- Increase self-knowledge
- Develop leadership skills

Because the kinds of outcomes associated with service-learning are not easily measured by objective tests, other forms of assessment are often adopted. You will probably be completing proof of learning that may be more work than simply studying for a test. These measures will give both you and your instructor a more complete picture of what you have learned throughout your experience and will show what you know and can do.

When you are invested in learning, you move from being a passive learner to being an active learner. Service-learning provides you with the opportunity to become not only an educated citizen, but also a thoughtful, active, socially conscious participant in society. Service-learning also helps you clarify the values and qualities of life that are important to you.

Maggie H., a first-year college student, facilitates leadership discussions with middle school girls in the YWCA Empowerment for Girls after-school program. In her journal she reflects:

> Each week that I work in the after-school program with the girls, I find out more and more about myself and what I value. Through the planned activities, we often end up discussing major social issues such as the environment, the influence of media on young girls, and diversity. The after-school program has become very important in my life because the goals of the program and our discussions help me clarify what I value and how these values can be reflected in my actions and behavior. The importance of service and being an informed citizen are qualities I hold in high regard. My service experience has made me aware of my role and responsibilities as a citizen.

# How Do I Know I Am Learning?

In your notebook, date and answer these questions periodically, starting before or early in your experience, returning midway through the experience, and returning again at the end of your experience. The changes and additions to your answers provide proof of your learning.

1. What new perspectives, other than my own (such as those of the community partner site director, the individual receiving services, a faculty member, or student affairs personnel), can I articulate with regard to the community issue?

2. What facts and statistics about the issue do I know?

3. What connections can I make between course theories or readings and my service experience?

4. What is my understanding of community and engaged citizenship as it relates to the issue with which I am involved?

5. How can I apply what I am learning about this issue in my own life, both now and in the future?

6. If asked, what would I tell others about what I am learning? How might I word this in a letter to the editor about the community issue or about service-learning as a teaching method?

Through her service experience, Maggie is developing valuable academic, social, and interpersonal skills that will help her adapt to the ever-changing world around her. To move her forward in the learning continuum, her facilitator may want to help Maggie articulate exactly what her values are, what she has discovered about living out those values, and how to deal with challenges to those values.

Because you will be interacting in community with others, you will always be dealing with values and worldviews, both your own and those of others. Therefore, you will need to find a way of reflecting and acting on the values and views that are important to you. Kevin LaNave, Coordinator of Service-Learning for St. Cloud Technical College, uses a three-step process to help students recognize what they are learning, how they are changing, and how to interact with the world:

1. Encountering and understanding "the way things are"
2. Evaluating "the way things are" in the light of some sense of "the way things ought to be"
3. Acting in ways that participate in a process of moving "the way things are" more fully toward "the way things ought to be"

Not everyone will have the same responses to these considerations. Taking time to reflect and to discuss them with others will reveal the richness of multiple perspectives and what you might learn from others.

LaNave suggests a conceptual framework to assist the development of value reflection:

• The idea of multiple perspectives, which often helps people transcend an either/or way of framing conversations about values
• The distinction between dialogue and debate
• The distinction between "subjective" and "objective" kinds of truth

This conceptual framework is intended to help you move through a value-reflection process when you are faced with challenges to your own values. Too often we insist on our own points of view without explicitly understanding the values we hold or how and why we developed those values. On the other hand, being too willing to accept all values and views as equal—what might be called the tendency toward total relativism—denies important realities. It is necessary to raise critical questions about values and perspectives that are not in harmony, but it is also crucial to learn where you stand on important issues and why. Significantly, service-learning provides the opportunity to practice value development and to put your values to the test.

Others share an interest in your learning, such as future service-learning students, your community partner, college administrators, your parents, college alumni, and perhaps especially your teacher. If you are participating in service-learning in a particular course, a significant portion of your overall grade will be determined by your service-learning work. Make sure that you

## Outcomes in a Variety of Courses

### Course: Natural Resource Management

**Outcome:** Students will demonstrate a comprehensive knowledge of assessing land use for outdoor recreation.

**Activity:** Conduct an ecological impact assessment of a proposed trail for the local community. Present results at a park board meeting.

### Course: Education

**Outcome:** Students will demonstrate the ability to create community support for educational programs.

**Activity:** Plan and implement a program involving key community leaders, administrators, parents, and children in a local school district.

### Course: Health Promotion

**Outcome:** Students will demonstrate the ability to develop promotion strategies to reach indigent populations.

**Activity:** Counsel migrant workers on the importance of conducting monthly testicular and breast self-examinations.

**Source:** Valerius and Hamilton.

understand what is required and what you are expected to produce through service-learning.

Studying a few models may help you appreciate both the significance and the valid expectations of the established outcomes. Look at the boxed examples of learning outcomes and the service-learning activities that are linked to those outcomes.

To challenge traditional ways of thinking about and assessing learning, service-learning practitioners apply a variety of processes for measuring learning. These processes include portfolios filled with student drawings, audio and/or video recordings, and other assignments completed throughout the term; individual and/or team projects; and exhibitions and/or presentations. Assessment tools also may include action taken by your instructor, the service-learning staff, or your community partner in cooperation with you, such as in-depth interviews, focus group surveys and/or interviews, and direct observation (Kezar 18–19). Andrew Furco's Evaluation System for Experiential Education (ESEE) is a model for service-learning outcomes and appropriate forms of assessment.

> The process includes a pretest and posttest survey instrument; journal questions; focus group interviews with students and faculty; content analysis of student work such as papers, portfolios, and presentations; a student placement questionnaire; teachers' program goals and objectives; classroom site visits and observations; and formal and informal meetings with site administrators. (Kezar 19)

## Outcomes Assessment Instruments

- Pretest and posttest surveys
- Journals
- Papers—essays, short stories, experiential research findings
- Portfolios including drawings, audio and/or video recordings, writing
- Individual or team project
- Exhibition (photography, art, short writings)
- Presentations
- Individual and/or focus group interviews

Furco's work provides a comprehensive look at an entire programmatic evaluation process, but we can extrapolate useful assessment techniques to get at the learning that occurs through the service-learning experience. A list of ways to demonstrate that the outcomes desired have been achieved appears in the Outcomes Assessment Instruments box.

Return to your syllabus and/or course notes, and review the learning outcomes that have been developed for your service-learning experience as well as the work you are expected to complete to achieve these outcomes. Can you see a direct connection between the desired outcomes and the instruments being used to evaluate your learning? By the end of your experience, you should have met these expectations.

**F**OCUS EXERCISE

**Matching Objectives and Service-Learning Activities**

In a small group, review the expectations that have been established for your service-learning experience. If objectives have been identified, discuss them. How do they match up with activities you will undertake? How will your behavior or action be assessed to assure that you have met the objectives? What evidence (such as pictures, artifacts, quotations from community partners) will you need to gather or provide to show that you are meeting the objectives? You might not have all the information needed to make a complete list of evidence, but you can add to this list as you do your work. Together, brainstorm other possible objectives and outcomes, including supporting evidence. Write at least one additional objective, and indicate how it could be assessed.

Though education is most clearly concerned with student learning, the service-learning method requires consideration of outcomes beyond student learning, such as the effect on those served and on the community issue with which you are dealing. How might you, your instructor, and your community partner assess the effect of your service? Besides measuring your success and efficacy, such assessment may help point the way to future service partnerships.

# Organizing for Service-Learning Success

Now that you understand the roles of the people involved in the service-learning experience as well as how the activities lead to learning outcomes, it is time to organize for success. Communication is key. The person responsible for facilitating the service-learning experience—your teacher, a student affairs administrator, or a campus coordinator—needs to communicate the expectations for the service-learning experience to you. These expectations include learning outcomes, the amount of service in hours, and follow-up reflection and activities. The same expectations should be communicated to your service site supervisor so that the on-site experience can be structured to both assist your community partner and allow learning success. In the best collaborative model of authentic partnership, your community partner, your instructor, and you will all play active roles in constructing the expectations. Since not all service-learning experiences or partnerships are identical, we emphasize the need for communication.

Your campus service-learning director or your instructor may choose to communicate directly with the site manager. However, you should follow up with the site manager to share information and discuss how the partnership can best benefit all involved. Prepare a folder of information for your site manager, keeping a copy for yourself. Include any contemplation activities or focus exercises that you have done to prepare for your service-learning experience, especially if they will help your community partner understand both what you have to offer and what you need to learn. For instance, the focus exercise in which you listed your abilities and skills and the areas in which you need to grow or learn could help the site supervisor direct your experience for maximum mutual benefit.

You may also want to discover whether other students are serving at the same site. Having a supportive peer group often helps. Because many service-learning sites may be beyond walking distance from your campus, you may want to carpool or use public transportation to get there. Traveling to the site with peers will let you discuss your experience and will assist you in deeper reflection on what you are learning and doing. If you have been struggling with a specific aspect of your service, talking with a peer may help you gain a different perspective. Of course, in any discussion, confidentiality and courtesy must be maintained.

Carpooling or using public transport is a civic responsibility in terms of both the environment and the economic aspects. The demand for oil may one day outrun supply, and fewer cars means a little less pollution. In many cities, parking is at a premium, too; the fewer cars that need to be parked, the better. Whether you carpool, use public transportation, or use some other form of transportation, be aware that you are responsible for your own choice about how you get to and from your site.

You will have opportunities beyond traveling to and from your site to discuss the shared experience with your peers. Your instructor or coordinator will likely set aside class or group time for such discussions. You may also be called upon to participate in wider community discussions based on your service-learning experience, such as a campus presentation followed by a question-and-answer session.

Perhaps the richest source for discussion will be your service-learning notebook. Even if your facilitator or instructor does not require such a notebook, you should keep one for your own benefit. Keep documents connected with the experience—site orientation materials, associated college documents, permissions, syllabus, service schedule, journal entries, concerns and questions to follow up on, and any other materials relevant to your experience.

Finally, to organize for success, you need to create a workable schedule that includes your commitment to service-learning. This is especially important if you also have a job, a family, a demanding course load, and/or cocurricular or extracurricular activities. Make a weekly schedule. Schedule commitments first: classes, job, and, of course, service-learning. To schedule your service-learning commitments, you will need to work cooperatively with your community partner. Take the partner's busy schedule into account, and adjust as possible. Next schedule study time, commitments to extracurricular or cocurricular activities, time with family and friends, and free time. If you keep to a schedule, you are less likely to procrastinate and more likely to experience success, and you will also have more time to enjoy life.

## Focus EXERCISE

### Checklist for Organizing for Success

Check off each item as you gather or complete it.

- ❑ **Folder for Site Supervisor**
  - ❑ Description of course
  - ❑ Learning objectives
  - ❑ Service tasks you have agreed to perform
  - ❑ List of your abilities and skills
  - ❑ Your desired areas for growth and learning
  - ❑ Your personal contact information
  - ❑ Agreed-on schedule for service
- ❑ **Service-Learning Notebook**
  - ❑ Site orientation materials (mission, history, brochures, directions, agency contacts, and so on)
  - ❑ College documents associated with service-learning
  - ❑ Permissions
  - ❑ Syllabus
  - ❑ Service schedule
  - ❑ Journal
  - ❑ Concerns and questions for follow-up
  - ❑ Other relevant materials
- ❑ **Weekly Schedule**
  - ❑ Classes
  - ❑ Job
  - ❑ Service-learning
  - ❑ Cocurricular or extracurricular activities
  - ❑ Family and friends time
  - ❑ Free time

## Focus EXERCISE

### Taking Stock of Your Preparedness

Are you prepared for success? What have you done to prepare for a successful service-learning experience? Make a list of the steps you have taken toward success. What are you most excited about? What are you feeling the most anxious about? Illustrate or write about your feelings. Share your excitement and anxiety with a peer involved in service-learning. How do sharing your feelings and hearing someone else's hopes and fears help prepare you?

Having taken these organizational steps, you will, we hope, have gained confidence that you are ready to enter the service-learning experience. To be great, leaders must be well organized. Through service-learning, you are moving from the student phase of life to active leadership, preparing to become a transformative community member.

# The CARC Learning Cycle: Contemplation, Action, Reflection, and Commitment

So far this text has discussed what service-learning is, why we do it, and what the various roles of the participants are. Now it is time to discuss exactly how to engage in service-learning. Basic to this discussion is the CARC Learning Cycle, a developmental process based on what the authors of this text have learned from past educators and theorists and what we have learned through practicing service-learning with our students.

The work of John Dewey in the first half of the twentieth century provided much of the foundation for today's practice of service-learning. Dewey did

#1

**LEARNING OBJECTIVES**

After studying this chapter and doing the exercises, you should be able to

- Define the four stages of the CARC Learning Cycle
- Recognize how to construct an attitudinal scale for the purposes of contemplation
- Identify the different forms of action or labor that you might be expected to do
- Discuss the usefulness of forked-road situations
- Identify the four C's of reflection
- Explain why commitment is an essential part of the citizenship model of service-learning

not use the term *service-learning*, but his philosophy of learning, experience, citizenship, and community helped shape today's service-learning pedagogy. Dewey pioneered the field of experiential learning, asserting that classroom learning accorded higher value to theory and ideas than to experience. He recognized the importance of interaction between life experiences and classroom

105

education, and he highly valued firsthand experience in close relationship with, not apart from, theory:

> An ounce of experience is better than a ton of theory simply because it is only in experience that any theory has vital and verifiable significance. An experience, a very humble experience, is capable of generating and carrying any amount of theory (or intellectual content), but a theory apart from an experience cannot be definitely grasped even as theory. It tends to become a mere verbal formula. (*Democracy and Education* 144)

Today Dewey's ideas form the foundation of the service-learning pedagogy with which you are involved. Service-learning advocates and researchers recognize the essential reciprocal relationship between experience and learning: "It is through active learning and the interplay between abstract, remote content and personal, palatable experiences that student learning is deepened and strengthened" (Bringle and Hatcher 114).

Other educational theorists, most notably David A. Kolb, extended Dewey's theory by emphasizing the importance of experience in learning: "Learning is the process whereby knowledge is created through the transformation of experience" (*Experiential Learning* 38). He identified a four-stage cycle (see Chapter 1), which has been further adapted by others. For example, Toole and Toole's Service-Learning Cycle draws on Kolb's work and emphasizes the importance of reflection opportunities before, during, and after service. Toole and Toole divide their cycle and reflection into three stages: preservice, during service, and postservice (99–114). The important ideas that Dewey, Kolb, and the Tooles have contributed to the practice of service-learning include the need for experiential learning, the critical role of reflection, and the notion that learning is both continuous and cyclical.

We call our adaptation of the experiential learning process the CARC Learning Cycle: Contemplation, Action, Reflection, and Commitment. While the Tooles divide their stages into before, during, and after reflection, we draw attention to the distinctively different types of thinking that occur during these stages: **Contemplation** (the before stage), **Action**, **Reflection** (during and immediately following action), and **Commitment** (the after stage).

The CARC graphic, which is shown in Figure 6.1, is shaped like a helix. The shape is metaphorically appropriate because it is also the shape of DNA, a spiral drill bit, and the common screw. Like DNA, this learning cycle represents the basic building blocks for the service-learning life. During your

## Focus Exercise

### Discussing Dewey's Assertion

Reflect on the quote from *Democracy and Education*. How does your experience confirm or challenge Dewey's assertion? Discuss this with your class or group.

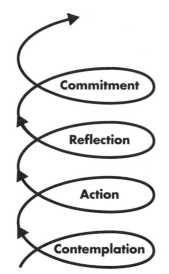

**FIGURE 6.1    The CARC Learning Cycle: Contemplation, Action, Reflection, and Commitment**

service-learning experience, you will use your problem-solving skills to drill through problems that you encounter. Just as the common screw holds structures together, the cyclical experience will strongly connect service and learning while connecting you with community partners in a reciprocal relationship. The discussion of the components of the cycle is set up in a linear fashion; but each aspect is continuously interwoven into the experience and may, at times, overlap with other aspects.

# Contemplation

Before going to your service site, you need *to deliberate consciously about the challenges, needs, and expectations of the service experience.* This deliberation is the *contemplation* aspect. Contemplation should take place before each time that you go to work at your service site. If you are journaling, you may want to write a contemplation entry in which you answer the following questions:

- What are my attitude and my energy level today?

- What skill, attitude, or idea do I need to work to develop today?

- What do I imagine or hope I might do, learn, and benefit from today as I interact with others? How might I engage in the reciprocal relationship of service?

Making these notes will help you focus your mind and your energy, make you more conscious of your own weaknesses or limitations, and help you have an attitude of openness to others. You will be more prepared to let the

encounter shape your understanding as you practice compassionate citizenship while working side-by-side with your community partners. Even though you are intentionally anticipating the encounter and what you may learn and do, you must remain open to surprise, both good and bad.

The purpose of anticipation in contemplation is to help you become more self-aware and socially attuned so that the serving and learning process will be enriched. According to Janet Eyler, who refers to this kind of contemplation as reflection **before** service, "Asking students to bring to the surface some of these thoughts in an explicit way before they perform their initial service may serve both as a benchmark for later reflection and an exercise that heightens their awareness of the frames of reference that they bring to the new experience. From the beginning, they may experience their service in a more reflective way" (36).

Students who have become experienced at contemplation as a part of the CARC Learning Cycle recognize the importance of the stage to the whole experience. Brittany K., a philosophy student, expressed it this way in her journal:

> In Book Ten, Chapter Seven [of *Nicomachean Ethics*], Aristotle says that contemplation is the highest human good. He also says that it is the most continuous activity, and because it is continuous, we as humans are more capable of it than we are of any continuous action. I think contemplation is the reason that service can be such a high value for me, or anyone for that matter. Nobody probably gets much out of committing to service unless they think about what they are giving and receiving. I believe that thinking about what you receive is just as important, if not more important, than what you give. It is from this contemplation that service begins to mean something, as Aristotle states.

For Brittany, contemplation sets up the intensity and the value of the service-learning experience. She is more prepared to both act and learn than is someone who does not practice contemplation.

You can practice contemplation on your own, with classmates, or with community partners. A particularly interesting and enlightening contemplation exercise that you can do on your own, preferably before your first day at the site, is Letter to Myself. Write a letter contemplating the experience to come, then seal it and leave it unopened until the end of your service-learning experience. After your last day at the site, reread your letter and reflect on how the entire service-learning experience has gone for your community partner and you, what service you have provided, what you have learned, and how you have grown. This contemplation exercise allows you to initiate critical thinking that will continue as you move through the entire CARC Learning Cycle.

A few guiding questions will help you structure your letter. Eyler, who also uses this activity, suggests the following:

- What will the people I will be working with be like?

- What will I contribute?

- What will I see in this part of my community? (37)

We add a few more to the list:

- What will I learn about the gifts and dreams of the people I encounter?
- What might it be like to "be in the shoes" of people I encounter?
- What is the most important thing that I hope to learn?
- How might this experience affect me?
- How might this experience influence my view of community?
- What will I discover about the causes and possible solutions of the community issue that is the focus of the service-learning experience?

Once you have reflected on the answers that have developed over the course of your experience, you may have excellent material for an essay or a larger project.

If you are in a group setting before your service-learning experience, you could benefit from group contemplation. If you are experiencing a mix of hope and fear, you may be certain that your peers are, too, though perhaps not the same hopes and fears. As a group, brainstorm the hopes and fears each has, writing the responses on an overhead, chalkboard, or flip chart. Return to this list after your service, and compare notes about the experience to launch a fruitful reflective discussion. It would also be helpful to either develop or review a set of learning objectives for the experience.

Some students who began service-learning during orientation week were not sure what the Hands for Change orientation experience meant. Two upper-class-student mentors and the faculty member in whose class they would continue

the service-learning experience gathered them together for contemplation before embarking on the initial site visit. The students learned that Hands for Change was an initial service-learning experience in which all incoming students participated. They were told that they would be going to a local recreation center that had been badly damaged by flooding the previous spring.

The group brainstormed about what they might encounter there, shared their own experiences of the flood, and created a series of learning objectives based on Bloom's Taxonomy moving from basic knowledge to the more complex skill of evaluation:

- Knowledge: learn the mission of the center and whom it serves

- Application: repair and renovate recreational space and materials to better serve the community

- Analysis: determine what is still left to be done to make the center fully operational (directly applicable to ongoing service during the semester)

- Evaluation: estimate the benefits gained by the community, the class, and each individual involved

Knowing the learning objectives helped the students understand what was expected and helped them observe, consider, and discover what they needed to learn. The students got their semester off to a good start by doing careful contemplation followed by action and reflection on that first day, with a commitment to follow through during the course.

Another group contemplation exercise that allows active involvement is the creation of a room-size attitudinal scale to measure attitudes and initial perspectives. Place the following descriptors around the room at well-spaced intervals: Strongly Agree, Agree, Neutral, Disagree, and Strongly Disagree. As a group, discuss how the room should be a safe space for all to express themselves honestly. All are on a journey and are perhaps at different places, which give you different perspectives. Find ways to nurture and value one another even when you disagree. No one should feel ostracized for holding an opinion, especially since perspectives change over time and with further experience.

After the discussion of a safe space, the group or the facilitator should come up with a series of statements related to the service-learning experience. As each statement is read, listen carefully, and then go to the descriptor that best correlates with your attitude, learning something about yourself and your group of peers in the process.

Had the students who were going to serve at the recreation center practiced such contemplation, the statements might have read as follows:

- "Recreation is not of much importance to the overall health and welfare of a community."

- "Community recreation centers make sports and recreation available on a more equitable basis, regardless of economic standing."

- "Recreation and sports teach values of teamwork and leadership."

- "Too much funding goes to recreation and sports at a time when finances are tight."

| STUDENT PARTICIPANT | COMMUNITY PARTNER |
|---|---|
| Learning Objectives: | Mission: |
| Skills: | Skills of Staff Members/Volunteers: |
| Talents: | Skills/Talents of Clients: |
| Interests: | Interests of the Organization: |
| Experience That I Bring: | Experience We Can Provide to You: |

**FIGURE 6.2   Service-Learning Asset Map**

After moving around the room, responding, and seeing how others respond, the group members should discuss how they reacted to the statements and why. Explicit awareness of your attitudes can help you learn where you have barriers or prejudices that you may need work to overcome or why you might feel already positively inclined to engage in certain types of service more than in others. Such awareness can help you monitor your thoughts as well as your speech and actions.

Finally, you may have the opportunity to engage in contemplation with your community partner. Perhaps the site supervisor or a staff member will meet with you before service so that you can practice asset mapping together.[1] You and your community partner should each draw up a list of the assets that you could provide to one another. Consider your skills, talents, interests, and experience. Your partner will need to consider the mission and interests of the organization, the skills of clients and individuals who already work or volunteer at the site, and experiences that it can provide you as you serve and learn (see Figure 6.2).

---

[1]In 1993 John P. Kretzmann and John L. McKnight began their groundbreaking work on "asset-based community development" with *Building Communities from the Inside Out: A Path Toward Finding and Mobilizing a Community's Assets*. Since then, these codirectors of the Asset-Based Community Development Institute at Northwestern University have written and spoken widely on the subject. Their initial book and subsequent publications provide many useful forms for mapping assets from various perspectives.

**F**OCUS EXERCISE

**Contemplating Your Service Experience**

Complete one of the contemplation exercises described in this chapter: Letter to Myself, the attitudinal scale, or asset mapping. Discuss with others how this exercise helps focus and prepare you for your service-learning activities.

When you have completed your individual inventories, compare notes and discuss how you might best serve one another and benefit from each other's assets. Taking this step will help you avoid the attitude that you are merely meeting needs for your partner and will help you recognize what your partner gives to you. When partnerships are built on appreciating one another's assets, real community is developed.

Engaging in this contemplative step will start your service-learning with greater meaning and connection. Remember, to be *contemplative* means *to consciously think deeply about an idea, an issue, or a task before taking action*. Thinking deeply together enhances the possibility for success in every way.

# Action

*Action* means *the on-site work that you undertake when matched with a community partner*. Types of work vary widely, depending on whether your service-learning is facilitated through an academic course, student affairs, or a college organization or club. If you are in a course, the action might also vary depending on whether the course is part of general education, the liberal arts, or your major or minor. You may provide physical labor, intellectual skills, or social and emotional support. To help you comprehend the many possibilities, take a look at the Examples of Service-Learning Action box.

You need to consider the appropriate dress and behavior associated with the kinds of service you are providing. Some behaviors will be expected regardless of the kind of labor in which you engage. You should always keep the commitments that you have made to your community partner. Make sure that you arrive at the time you are expected and that you report to the appropriate staff member. Always practice courtesy in all relationships—with administrators and staff members, other community volunteers, and clients. Listen carefully, speak respectfully, and guide gently. As a sign of respect, address adults by the appropriate titles and surnames unless they ask you to use their given names. Maintain confidentiality, even when writing about site experiences; use pseudonyms for clients and coworkers, or use other appropriate measures for guarding identities (initials, numbers, abbreviated forms of names). Follow all rules and regulations established by the community partner, as well as those of your college.

# Examples of Service-Learning Action

## Physical Labor

- Earn general education credit in health and wellness by building playground equipment and creating toys and games for a low-income daycare center.

- Participate in an alternative spring break by joining your residence hall in building homes for Habitat for Humanity, focusing on the meaning of *home* and *residence*.

- As a part of your dietetics major, serve at a local food pantry once a week, stocking shelves and preparing food packages for clients. Take such special needs as ethnicity, religion, and medical conditions into consideration.

## Intellectual Skills

- Earn general education credits in a foreign language, English, or math by tutoring children at a local school twice a week.

- As a member of the English Club, Scribes and Scrolls, lead weekly book discussions for community members, helping them interpret passages and develop a love for reading.

- As a computer science major, partner with a local computer support company to provide support and technology training to nonprofit organizations.

## Social and Emotional Support

- As a first-year student in an introductory liberal arts course focused on "the examined life," visit your Adopt-a-Grandparent elder once a week for conversation and social activities, learning life lessons in the process.

- As a member of the social justice club, be matched with a buddy with developmental problems by an organization such as ARC, and take your buddy on weekly public outings that will help socially affirm his or her value and provide greater social skills and confidence.

- As a gender studies major, work with the Empowerment of Girls YWCA program on a weekly basis to mentor young women and help them develop confidence and strategies for success.

In some instances, you may be required to undergo training before contact with the community partner or its clients. For instance, if you serve at a rape and abuse crisis center, you will likely require several hours' to two weeks' worth of training before your first service experience. This is an important part of your learning and is sometimes a legal requirement as well. Probably all partners, as well as your campus facilitator, will expect you to go through an on-site orientation session at least. This session gives you the opportunity to learn about the mission, the staff members and their duties, and the physical space and setup. It is an ideal time to ask pertinent questions. Throughout the action

> ❗ **SERVICE-LEARNING ACTION TIPS**
>
> ✔ Arrive promptly at the time you are expected
> ✔ Dress appropriately
>   - **Physical labor:** jeans (neither too tight nor too loose), shoes with good support (work boots, walking shoes), work gloves, bandana
>   - **Intellectual labor:** nice slacks and shirt; skirt, dress, or dress pants
>   - **Social and emotional support:** clothing suitable to the day's activity
> ✔ Follow the rules and regulations set by community partner and/or college
> ✔ Address adults by appropriate titles and surnames until directed otherwise
> ✔ Listen attentively, using eye contact and receptive body language
> ✔ Speak and act with courtesy, respect, and confidentiality
> ✔ Ask questions and seek direction as needed

**FOCUS EXERCISE**

**Recording Your Action and Learning**

Immediately following your on-site action, record exactly what you did that day. What kind of labor did you provide: physical, intellectual, or social and emotional? What happened this day that particularly struck you? Later you will return to this record to reflect on how you contributed and what you learned about yourself and the community.

aspect of your service-learning experience, ask questions as they arise and seek direction when necessary.

It is likely that you already have a designated community partner and some notion of what your activity will be. However, if you are given a choice, review your skills and learning needs as well as community assets and needs before choosing. If you have the opportunity to explore various agencies—perhaps by attending a service-learning fair or talking with service-learning staff or students who have previously participated—you may be able to make a more informed choice. A brainstorming session could help you select the most beneficial activity for both the wider community and your own growth and development. You may engage in more than one type of activity for your community partner, depending on the length of time you are serving and learning and the success of your joint inventory of the assets you bring. The action you take now will likely lead to ongoing service and learning for life, a natural part of your engaged citizenship.

# Reflection    #6

Chapter 1 introduced you to four central traits that characterize service-learning: a commitment to serve genuine community needs, an emphasis on academic learning and rigor, an expectation of intentional reflective thinking, and the opportunity to foster civic responsibility. While all four tenets contribute to a meaningful service-learning experience, intentional reflective thinking provides the critical link between your service, the desired learning outcomes, and the development of civic responsibility.

Your professor or service-learning facilitator has planned opportunities for critical reflection to help you achieve the desired learning goals. As discussed in Chapter 4, critical thinking includes abstract, creative, and systematic thinking as well as precise communication. Given the broad ramifications, it is important to understand how essential reflection is to your learning because it calls for you to do complex processing.

Reflection helps you process your service actions and connect them with your learning goals. Simply stated, *reflection is the lens through which you think critically about the experience, deeply considering how the action intentionally links to specific learning goals.* There is no single way to reflect on your service-learning experience; rather, there are many different, sometimes creative ways. Your professor or facilitator may assign a specific method of reflection or may ask your community partner or an expert in the field to assist you in practicing meaningful reflection. Other times, you may be required to create a reflection strategy that is appropriate to your service site and that suits the learning objectives. Therefore, it is important to have a sound understanding of the reflection phase of the CARC Learning Cycle.

Working at your service site doesn't necessarily translate to achieving your learning objectives or heightening your sense of social responsibility. Rather, intentional, well-timed reflection connects your concrete service experience to the desired outcomes. Informally talking with others about your experience is not considered adequate reflection because informal conversations, no matter how meaningful, do not provide structured critical thinking opportunities that intentionally connect your actions with the learning goals. Structured reflection continually challenges your thinking and enhances your learning. As Dewey puts it, "Thought or reflection . . . is the discernment of the relation between what we try to do and what happens in consequence. No experience having a meaning is possible without some element of thought" (*Democracy and Education* 144–145). Reflection is the essential bridge between your lived experiences and authentic learning. Because of this, it is always central to the pedagogy of service-learning.

For instance, Sophie G., a student who served in the YWCA Empowerment of Girls program, recorded the following after a discussion of the importance of women's history month and specific women who have changed history:

> It is very important for girls to see what women in the past have done to affect our world today. I could see how much the girls enjoyed the conversation today

because they said they were learning things about women that hadn't been covered in their history classes. Through our discussions today about women like Rosa Parks and Margaret Thatcher, we all came to better understand how one woman can help change the course of other women's lives even generations later. In fact, this is exactly what the Empowerment of Girls program strives to do—to make connections among women across time. I am glad I just realized that—it was one of those light-bulb moments for me.

As it did for Sophie, reflection can illuminate issues that go beyond the initial service experience, connecting your action to the wider society.

At times throughout your service-learning experience you will probably have feelings of doubt, uncertainty, and even frustration. Reflective thinking can help you work through such challenges. Dewey recognized the potential for thinking and growth in times of perplexity: "Thinking begins in what may fairly enough be called a *forked-road* situation, a situation that is ambiguous, that presents a dilemma, that proposes alternatives" (*How We Think* 14).

Alysson G., an education student, encountered a difficult situation while tutoring in an after-school elementary math program:

Several times I've heard my fellow tutors say the most frustrating thing about tutoring is working with a student who is obviously trying so hard to understand a concept or idea, but simply can't understand it. I had such an experience today. I worked with a little girl who was quite shy and obviously not comfortable with working on her math homework with a complete stranger. . . . I tried explaining the necessary process for figuring out the addition problems she had been assigned, but she just stared at me blankly as if I were speaking another language. I was so frustrated that I wondered what I was even doing trying to tutor others.

This student is experiencing a significant amount of frustration and doubt. Reflection allows her to move beyond this moment of perplexity:

> After a day like this, I can truly appreciate what teachers must go through with their students on a daily basis. Not only do they potentially have to deal with rowdy students, but they also have to try to make sure all their students are grasping the day's lessons and material. I hadn't really thought about the wide range of learners in any given classroom. From my service experience today, I have come to understand what it takes to truly learn something—and all the factors that might affect a child's learning. My frustration with tutoring that little girl helped me examine the whole issue of student learning from perspectives other than my own. But now I'm questioning—how did this little girl slip through the cracks in our educational system? How is she going to catch up with her peers? What's her future going to be like if she can't add at even a third grade level? I'm also wondering how No Child Left Behind is going to help a student like this.

The process of thinking about and working through forked-road situations will lead you to new insights and informed actions because the "demand for the solution of a perplexity is the steadying and guiding factor of the entire process of reflection" (Dewey, *How We Think* 14). Dewey valued the key role that reflective thought plays in resolving ambiguities and perplexities: "The function of reflective thought is, therefore, to transform a situation in which there is experienced obscurity, doubt, conflict, disturbance of some sort, into a situation that is clear, coherent, settled, harmonious" (100–101).

Today's theorists share Dewey's assertion that reflection plays a central role in deepening thinking, achieving learning goals, and leading to committed action. Summarizing the Giles and Eyler studies, Bringle and Hatcher conclude: "When reflection activities engage the learner in dialogue and other forms of communication about the relationship between relevant, meaningful service and the interpretative template of a discipline, there is enormous potential for learning to broaden and deepen along academic, social, moral, and civic dimensions" (181). In short, reflection not only helps illuminate the current experience, but it may also help you discover a deeper sense of your calling, of how to use your gifts to act in the world.

While the reflection stage of the CARC Learning Cycle may take many different forms, quality reflection activities share four important traits, often known as the four C's of reflection: "effective critical reflection is Continuous, Connected, Challenging, and Contextualized" (Eyler, Giles, and Schmiede 16). As your service-learning facilitator guides you through the reflection process, attend to these key principles of reflection.

According to Eyler, Giles, and Schmiede, quality reflection is continuous on two levels. First, ideally, reflection should continue throughout your four-year educational career and even throughout your lifetime. If you seek out additional opportunities for contemplation, action, reflection, and commitment through service experiences, critical reflection will become your lifelong way

> ## ! SUGGESTIONS TO GUIDE SUCCESSFUL CRITICAL REFLECTION
>
> ✔ Capture the moment. Reflect on your service actions while experiences are fresh in your mind. Whenever possible, revisit your reflection later to think critically about your service to see if you have more to add.
>
> ✔ Stretch yourself in new ways. Try different forms of reflection (see the A Variety of Reflection Strategies sidebar). Take risks with your thinking. You are most likely to move to a deeper level of thinking when you encounter and work through forked-road situations.
>
> ✔ Develop a keen sense of observation. While at your site, pay attention to details—to the sights and sounds, to what others say and don't say, to what others do and don't do. Try to use as many of your five physical senses as possible when writing about your experience.
>
> ✔ Consider multiple perspectives. Examine your service setting, the circumstances, events, and tasks from the perspectives of others, not just your own perspective. Where and how do you fit in the service context?
>
> ✔ Use a full range of thought and feeling as you respond to your experiences. Explore your intellectual, emotional, and analytical thoughts about the experiences. Be conscious of what is happening inside of you.
>
> ✔ Make connections to course content, previous learning, and other life experiences.

of seeing, thinking about, and experiencing the world as a responsible citizen. The second way that effective reflection should be continuous is specific to your current service-learning experience (17). The CARC cycle emphasizes the cyclical and continual movement of your learning and thus the necessity of ongoing reflection. You might want to answer the following questions as part of your continuous reflection: How did my contemplation focus affect my action this day? As I reflect, what commitment do I want to make about my future service actions in order to more fully meet my learning objectives?

Connected reflection, the second principle of effective critical reflection according to Eyler, Giles, and Schmiede, emphasizes that reflection should provide powerful opportunities to connect service to the intended learning, often expressed in the learning objectives. Concrete service experiences are incorporated to help you challenge and understand the course readings, theories, and concepts in practical situations. Effective reflection also connects your service-learning experiences to broader understandings of community and active citizenship: "The synthesis of action and thought results from connected reflection" (Eyler, Giles, and Schmiede 18).

Ask yourself what connections you can make between your course readings and your service experience. For instance, students reading *Of Mice and Men* who are working with developmentally disabled partners might draw connections between how Lennie behaves and is treated in the novel and how their partner behaves and is treated in the community. You might even think about connections to your major and/or vocation. Regardless of whether a direct connection may be made, practicing connected reflection will help you realize how much you are learning and how this learning has application in your life. At the least, your learning connects to your civic preparation and prepares you for responsible leadership.

Challenging reflection, the third C of effective reflection, emphasizes that the reflection must challenge you to new ways of thinking: "one of the most critical components of effective reflection is . . . the practice of challenging students to engage issues in a more critical way" (Eyler, Giles, and Schmiede 19). Knowing this may help you understand your professor's high expectations for your reflective thinking throughout the service-learning cycle. Your service-learning facilitator has designed reflective opportunities to help you grow and learn from the experience. Intentional, structured, critical reflection should stretch you to new ways of thinking. You might confront assumptions, explore alternatives, question perceptions, raise issues, test theories, develop action plans, and ask difficult questions. As the nationally known community activist Sweet Alice Harris, who has devoted her life to helping the people of inner-city Watts, often says to students who work with her, "You have to go through it to get to it."

Finally, effective reflection is contextualized. Eyler, Giles, and Schmiede explain that "contextualized reflection is appropriate for the setting and context of a particular service-learning course or program; the environment and method of reflection corresponds in a meaningful way to the topics and experiences that form the material for reflection" (20). In other words, your professor or facilitator has incorporated reflection opportunities that are appropriate for the specific course or program learning objectives. In addition, specific reflection methods are designed for your particular learning context and are based on topics and issues that emerge from your service experience to help you develop the abilities to analyze, synthesize, and problem solve: "Reflection, when it is purposefully implemented in an appropriate and meaningful context, adds to the richness of the synthesis between thinking and doing" (Eyler, Giles, and Schmiede 20). To better reflect on your context, ask how the location of your service has influenced the choices your instructor or facilitator has made about what you should be learning and how you should go about providing evidence.

Now that you are beginning to appreciate the complex process of reflection, read the reflection of a premed student and see how he comes to recognize the way in which reflection deepens his understanding of his service and his learning. Here is what Casey N., who helped the chaplain at the veterans hospital prepare a weekly ecumenical worship service for patients and their families, had to say:

> There wasn't ever a point in my service at the VA where I thought my work wasn't valuable, but it was only at the end of the semester that I fully understood how many different roles I played and the importance of the roles. In the beginning of my time at the VA, I thought that I was simply helping set up for a chapel service— and that was about it. After serving for many weeks, however, I grew in my service through the careful reflection about my actions. The reflections helped me realize that my service was valued because of the many things I did well beyond

simply setting up for the service, such as interacting with the patients. As I look back through my reflection journal entries, I see that in going through not only the actions but also thinking critically about all that I did, I gained new understandings.

As Casey affirms, reflection is central to a quality service-learning experience.

The sidebar lists examples of various methods of reflection. Although the methods are listed as separate categories, many can be combined or adapted to various learning contexts. We all have different learning styles and preferences and different strengths, and some of the reflection activities may be more suitable for you than others. If you have the opportunity to select your own reflection method, explore a wide range of possibilities to find one that best suits your service and your strengths. However, it is important to keep stretching, to develop your capacity to learn in a variety of ways and styles. Your professor or facilitator will provide additional guidelines to tailor your reflection activities so they are continuous, connected, challenging, and contextualized.

Different reflection methods may also be used with different audiences. For example, you would write differently for your fellow service-learning participants, the service agency, your professor, and the broader community. Some of these individuals may use your reflections to help assess your learning. Reflection that can be used to educate others or raise consciousness in the wider community is appropriate for a wider audience. Regardless of audience, your task is to be as thorough and honest as possible in order to learn more and become a more complete human being.

## A Variety of Reflection Strategies

### Reflection through Writing

- Individual, paired, or group journals
- Formal essay or research paper
- Publication—pamphlet, letter, etc.—for the service agency
- Publication for the broader community, such as a newspaper article or letter to the editor
- Creative work such as a short story or poetry
- Collection and write-up of oral history based on interviews
- Written response to some type of directed reading
- Project report
- Case studies

### Reflection through Speaking and Listening

- Panel discussion
- Small-group or large-group discussions

- Class presentations
- Guest speaker and follow-up discussion or response
- Public speaking or community presentation
- Scenarios for discussion

## Reflection through Performing and Creative Arts

- Role playing or simulation activity
- Acting out a scene or situation
- Conducting a mock trial
- Readers theatre
- Teaching or presenting to another audience
- Interpretive dance
- Composing music
- Collage
- Photography or photographic essay
- Drawing
- Sculpture

## Reflection through Multimedia and Technology

- Trifold storyboard (a freestanding three-paneled presentation board)
- Scrapbook
- Presentation software
- Documentary video
- Web bulletin boards
- Chat rooms
- Class listserv or discussion boards
- Webpage design
- Digital storytelling through image and sound

## FOCUS EXERCISE

### Practicing Reflection

To help you explore a wide range of reflection options, choose two methods of reflection from two different categories and reflect on your service-learning experience. Compare the strengths and limitations of the types of reflection for your particular experience.

# Commitment

Commitment is a very real part of the entire experience in the CARC Learning Cycle. When you have **contemplated** carefully about learning goals and the service process, have **acted** to serve and to learn, and have **reflected** deeply on the outcomes, it is increasingly likely that you will find yourself **committing** to further service. The entire cycle will begin again as you contemplate your next way of serving and learning. You may even make a lifetime commitment. In *Where's the Learning in Service-Learning?* Janet Eyler and Dwight E. Giles indicate that service-learning has a significant "impact on students' belief in the importance of volunteering" (158). They are more likely to commit to service in their communities throughout their lives, choosing employment that connects to such service and/or volunteering in their communities. They are also more likely to understand and act on the connection between political engagement and civic responsibility. (To remind yourself of the variety of commitment possibilities, review the Social Change Wheel at the end of Chapter 3).

In this context, *commitment* means *a disciplined effort to act on your belief in the communal necessity of service and in the benefits it affords all involved.* While you are continuing your service-learning experience, you will feed that commitment into contemplating how to improve your service action and reflective learning. Beyond this experience, you will need to know how to choose where, when, and how to serve to maximize the benefits for your community partners and your own growth. As Eyler and Giles note, "It is not enough to feel committed to community. Students also need the expertise and cognitive capacity to make intelligent decisions about what

needs to be done" (159). If you desire to serve but are unsure about your decision, do assessment mapping of your own skills and needs as well as of community assets and needs. Then look for the best match for the most beneficial service.

You might want to do a projection exercise at the end of your service-learning experience to help you ascertain your next step of commitment. In a course studying how personal values are created, students were given a choice of service opportunities. The instructor asked them to complete end-of-course displays that pulled all their service and learning together. They were to use a trifold board as follows:

- Panel 1: Choose three values that you have learned are critically important in the construction of community and in your own life. Define each value in your own words. Explain why that value is central to your life and how it is connected to an issue in contemporary society.

- Panel 2: Select excerpts from at least three of the texts that we have studied to illustrate each value. Also treat service-learning as a text, as a resource from which you are learning. Interpret the excerpts, and connect them to the corresponding value.

- Panel 3: Make a commitment to live out each value in community in the future. Detail how you will practice this commitment in both the short term and the long term.

The majority of students either used service as a value or used a correlation, such as generosity, that would call for a commitment to service within the community.

For example, Brittany K., whose essay on the need for contemplation was reprinted earlier, chose service as one of her three values and followed through on it:

- Definition: I believe that the definition of true service differs from volunteering. Volunteering is helping someone for a short period of time. In service, you make a commitment to continue helping people or organizations. When you value service, it means that you value helping people or organizations, and that you also contemplate what you are receiving in return for your service.
- Why It Is Important to Me: Before I began class, I had volunteered numerous times. I never truly committed to service before I began the Adopt-a-Grandparent program. This was a long-term commitment that made me realize not only am I helping numerous people, I am also gaining satisfaction, among numerous other things. Now that class is nearly finished, I still intend to visit my adopted grandma. Because of service, I have gained a new companion. I never really realized how much can be gained out of service. Now that I know, I intend to continue this path of helping other people while gaining experience and knowledge.

After this introduction on the first panel, Brittany connected the value of service to contemporary societal problems like long-term hurricane relief and repair in New Orleans. She also discussed service-learning as a valuable text in the class. Finally, she made short-term and long-term commitments in what she called her Plan of Action:

- I will continue to visit my adopted grandmother even after I am done with service-learning.
- I also plan to sign up for another service-learning event for one semester next year. It will be a different program than the Adopt-a-Grandparent program because I would like to further my experience in different types of service.
- One thing I consistently already do and plan to keep doing is helping out with my local church youth group. Even though I am too old to actually be in youth group, I still help out with their activities.
- I would like to make it my goal to keep participating in service-learning events even after next year.

Through service-learning, Brittany has recognized that a fulfilling life includes a commitment to service across her lifetime. She has made a plan for the next couple of years, and the likelihood is strong that she will continue such commitment into the distant future.

Commitments are serious matters, which is why one must be disciplined in order to fulfill them. Desire alone is not enough. There may be days when you do not feel like going to your service site; but if you are committed you will go.

Commitment enriches both your community partners and your own life. Again and again, students admit in contemplation sections of their journals that they did not feel like going to serve on a particular day—they were too tired, too stressed—but they planned on going anyway. The follow-up record of their actions and reflection always tells a different story, generally beginning: "I am so glad that I went today because . . ." Community partnerships, especially those combining service and learning, require dedication and commitment if they are to truly create and sustain positive relationships resulting in mutual benefits.

Part of the commitment that the authors of this book have made is to share what we have learned as we have worked alongside our service-learning

## FOCUS EXERCISE

### Projecting a Commitment to Service

Think of a population or group in your community to which you feel a strong allegiance or about which you feel deeply concerned (for example, the arts community, local or start-up businesses, children, the developmentally disabled, the elderly). Write the name of the group in the center of a piece of paper. Now create a web of connections that maps the assets and needs of that group.

Write your name in the middle of a second piece of paper. Now map your own assets and needs. Look for connections.

Write a one-page commitment that explains why you have chosen this group, how you plan to serve the group in the future, and what the group will bring to your life that will enrich it and that will help you learn and grow.

students and community partners. Your own journey will be unique to you; the way you contemplate, act, and reflect will shape your commitment to a lifelong calling to serve community. All that you do, know, and come to be by the end of your service-learning experience will also be shaped by and will contribute to the communities of which you are a part. We are all partners in society. Our individual and communal connectedness and effort make hope possible. A great American poet, Marianne Moore, has said what is possible in a powerful few lines:

**I May, I Might, I Must**

If you will tell me why the fen

appears impassable, I then

will tell you why I think that I

can get across it if I try.

This poem speaks to an invincible spirit with the ability to do and act in the face of difficult odds. Service-learning puts this same spirit into practice.

# Works Cited

AmeriCorps. "AmeriCorps NCCC: Service through Teamwork." *Serving Communities and Country*. 26 May 2006.
<http://www.americorps.org/about/programs/nccc.asp>.

———. "AmeriCorps VISTA: Helping Others Help Themselves." *Serving Communities and Country*. 26 May 2006. <http://www.americorps.org/about/programs/vista.asp>.

———. "What Is AmeriCorps?" *Serving Communities and Country*. 26 May 2006.
<http://www.americorps.org/about/ac/index.asp>.

Aristotle. *Nicomachean Ethics*. Trans. Terence Irwin. 2nd ed. Indianapolis: Hackett, 1999.

Association of American Colleges and Universities. *Greater Expectations: A New Vision for Learning as a Nation Goes to College*. Washington: Association of American Colleges and Universities, 2002.

Astin, Helen S., and Alexander W. Astin. *A Social Change Model of Leadership Development Guidebook*. Los Angeles: University of California, Higher Education Research Institute, 1996.

Atherton, James S. "The Experiential Learning Cycle." 2005. *Learning and Teaching* Doceo. 12 March 2006.
<http://www.learningandteaching.info/learning/experience.htm>.

Autry, James A. *The Servant Leader: How to Build a Creative Team, Develop Great Morale, and Improve Bottom Line Performance*. New York: Three Rivers, 2004.

Barber, Benjamin R. "Neither Leaders nor Followers: Citizenship under Strong Democracy." *Education for Democracy*. Ed. Benjamin R. Barber and Richard M. Battistoni. Dubuque: Kendall/Hunt, 1993. 161–170.

Barber, Benjamin R., and Richard M. Battistoni, eds. *Education for Democracy*. Dubuque: Kendall/Hunt, 1993.

Beer, Jennifer E. "Communicating across Cultures." *Culture at Work*. 14 January 2006.
<http://www.culture-at-work.com/highlow.html>.

Bereiter, Carl, and Marlene Scardamalia. "Intentional Learning as a Goal of Instruction." *Knowing, Learning, and Instruction: Essays in Honor of Robert Glaser*. Ed. Lauren B. Resnick. Hillsdale, NJ: Erlbaum, 1989. 361–392.

Bloom, Benjamin S. *Taxonomony of Educational Objectives, The Classification of Educational Goals, Handbook I: Cognitive Domain*. New York: David McKay, 1956. Rpt. In *Bloom's Taxonomy: A Forty-Year Retrospective*. Eds. Lorin W. Anderson and Lauren A. Sosniak. Chicago: University of Chicago, 1994. 9–27.

Boyte, Harry. "Practical Politics." *Education for Democracy*. Ed. Benjamin R. Barber and Richard M. Battistoni. Dubuque: Kendall/Hunt, 1993. 171–178.

Break Away. "Alternative Breaks." *Break Away: The Alternative Break Connection*. 4 April 2006. <http://alternativebreaks.org/Alternative_Breaks.asp>.

Bricker-Jenkins, Mary, Sarah Frohock, and Laura Rodgers. "Welcome to the School for Social Workers." *University of the Poor: Educational Arm of the Poor People's Economic Human Rights Campaign*. 7 June 2006.
<http://www.universityofthepoor.org/schools/social/welcome.html#>.

Bringle, Robert G., and Julie A. Hatcher. "Reflection in Service-Learning: Making Meaning of Experience." *Educational Horizons* Summer 1999: 179–185.

Buechner, Frederick. *Wishful Thinking: A Seeker's ABC*. San Francisco: Harper, 1993.

Campus Compact. "College Students Launch Month of Community Service and Civic Action." *Raise Your Voice: Student Action for Change*. 12 February 2006. <http://www.actionforchange.org/>.

———. "Our Vision, Mission, and Organizational Statements." *Educating Citizens, Building Communities*. 17 March 2006. <http://www.compact.org/about/mission>.

———. "Record Numbers of Colleges and Universities Are Making Community Service a Top Priority." *Compact.org*. 2006. 22 Feb. 2006. <http://www.compact.org/news/news-detail.php?viewstory=3279>.

Career Center. "What Are the Best Career Options for Me?" *Career Center*. 10 February 2006. <http://career.berkeley.edu/Plan/Option.stm>.

Chamberlain, Craig. "Teaching Teamwork: Project-Based Service-Learning Course LINCs Students with Nonprofits." *Inside Illinois*. 2003. 12 June 2006. <http://www.news.uiuc.edu/II/03/0123/linc.html>.

Colby, Anne, Thomas Ehrlich, Elizabeth Beaumont, and Jason Stephens. *Educating Citizens: Preparing America's Undergraduates for Lives of Moral and Civic Responsibility*. San Francisco: Jossey-Bass, 2003.

Cone, Richard, David D. Cooper, and Elizabeth L. Hollander. "Voting and Beyond: Engaging Students in Our Representative Democracy." *About Campus* 6.1 (2001): 2–8.

Coplin, Bill. *10 Things Employers Want You to Learn in College: The Know-How You Need to Succeed*. Berkeley: Ten Speed, 2003.

Cornwell, Grant H., and Eve W. Stoddard. *Globalizing Knowledge: Connecting International and Intercultural Studies*. The Academy in Transition Ser. 4. Washington: AACU, 1999.

Dewey, John. *Democracy and Education: An Introduction to the Philosophy of Education*. 1916. New York: Macmillan, 1944.

———. *How We Think: A Restatement of the Relation of Reflective Thinking to the Educative Process*. 1933. Boston: Houghton Mifflin, 1998.

Dubrin, Andrew J. *Leadership: Research Findings, Practice, and Skills*. 4th ed. New York: Houghton Mifflin, 2004.

EFF Center for Training and Technical Assistance. "EFF Standards Wheel." *Equipped for the Future Teaching/Learning Toolkit*. 30 March 2006. <http://eff.cls.utk.edu/toolkit/default.htm>.

Ellingboe, Brenda J. "Interpersonal Communication Skills for the Work Place." *Be Globally Focused*. 2000. 16 June 2006. <http://www.begloballyfocused.net/interpersonalskills.htm>.

Enelow, Wendy S., and Louise M. Kursmark. *Expert Resumes for Career Changers*. Indianapolis: JIST Works, 2005.

Enos, Sandra L., and Marie L. Troppe. "Service-Learning in the Curriculum." *Service-Learning in Higher Education: Concepts and Practices*. Eds. Barbara Jacoby and associates. San Francisco: Jossey-Bass, 1996. 156–181.

Eyler, Janet. "Creating Your Reflection Map." *New Directions for Higher Education* 114 (Summer 2001): 35–43.

Eyler, Janet, and Dwight E. Giles. *Where's the Learning in Service-Learning?* San Francisco: Jossey-Bass, 1999.

Eyler, Janet, Dwight E. Giles, Jr., and Charlene J. Gray. "Research at a Glance: What We Know about the Effects of Service-Learning on Students, Faculty, Institutions, and Communities, 1993–1999." *Introduction to Service-Learning Toolkit: Readings and Resources for Faculty*. Providence: Campus Compact, 2000. 19–22.

Eyler, Janet, Dwight E. Giles, and Angela Schmiede. *A Practitioner's Guide to Reflection in Service-Learning: Student Voices and Reflections*. Nashville: Vanderbilt U, 1996.

Figler, Howard E., Carol Carter, Joyce Bishop, and Sarah Lyman Kravits. *Keys to Liberal Arts Success*. Upper Saddle River, NJ: Prentice Hall, 2002.

Gardner, John N., and A. Jerome Jewler. *Step by Step to College and Career Success*. Boston: Thomson Wadsworth, 2006.

Gilmore, Richard. "Propaedeutic for Teaching Aristotle's *Nicomachean Ethics*." Principia Faculty Workshop. Concordia College-Moorhead, MN. Summer 2003.

"The Goals for Liberal Learning." Concordia College-Moorhead, MN. 16 January 2004. <http://www4.cord.edu/acadAffairs/reports/Goals20040116.pdf>.

Greenleaf Center for Servant-Leadership. "What Is Servant-Leadership?" 29 June 2006. <http://www.greenleaf.org/leadership/servant-leadership/What-is-Servant-Leadership.html>.

Halford, Joan Montgomery. "A Different Mirror: A Conversation with Ronald Takaki." *Educational Life: Understanding Race, Class and Culture* 56. 7 (April 1999): 8–13. 4 October 2005. <http://www.ascd.org/ed_topics/el199904_halford.html>.

Hoover, Eric. "Freshman Survey: More Students Plan to Lend a Hand." *Chronicle of Higher Education* 52.22 (2006): A40–A41. *Chronicle.com*. 3 Feb. 2006. <http://chronicle.com/weekly/v52/i22/22a04001.htm>.

Irwin, Terence. Introduction. *Nicomachean Ethics*. By Aristotle. Trans. Terence Irwin. 2nd ed. Indianapolis: Hackett, 1999. xiii–xxviii.

Kezar, Adrianna. "Assessing Community Service-Learning: Are We Identifying the Right Outcomes?" *About Campus* May–June 2002: 14–20.

Kivel, Paul. "How White People Can Serve as Allies to People of Color in the Struggle to End Racism." *White Privilege: Essential Readings on the Other Side of Racism*. Ed. Paula S. Rothenberg. New York: Worth, 2002. 127–135.

Kivisto, Peter. *Multiculturalism in a Global Society*. 21st Century Sociology Ser. Oxford: Blackwell, 2002.

Kolb, David A. *Experiential Learning: Experience as the Source of Learning and Development*. Englewood Cliffs, NJ: Prentice Hall, 1984.

——. "Learning Styles and Disciplinary Differences." *The Modern American College: Responding to the New Realities of Diverse Students and a Changing Society*. Ed. Arthur W. Chickering. San Francisco: Jossey-Bass, 1981. 232–255.

Kretzmann, John P., and John L. McKnight. *Building Communities from the Inside Out: A Path toward Finding and Mobilizing a Community's Assets*. Chicago: ACTA, 1993.

LaNave, Kevin. "Social Justice—It's Like 'Looking in the Mirror.'" Presented at multiple workshops. Provided to authors via e-mail 30 May 2006.

LeBaron, Michelle. "Communication Tools for Understanding Cultural Differences." *Beyond Intractability: A Free Knowledge Base on More Constructive Approaches to Destructive Conflict*. 2003. 16 January 2006. <http://www.beyondintractability.org/essay/communication>.

LeFasto, Frank, and Carl Larson. *When Teams Work Best: 6,000 Team Members and Leaders Tell What It Takes to Succeed*. Thousand Oaks: Sage, 2001.

Levine, Arthur, and Jeanette S. Cureton. *When Hope and Fear Collide: A Portrait of Today's College Students*. San Francisco: Jossey-Bass, 1998. 157–160.

Levine, Mel. "College Graduates Aren't Ready for the Real World." *The Chronicle of Higher Education* 52. 24 (18 Feb. 2005): B11. July 2005. <http://chronicle.com/weekly/v51/i24/24b01101.htm>.

Levinas, Emmanuel. *Entre Nous: Thinking-of-the-Other*. Trans. Michael B. Smith and Barbara Harshav. New York: Columbia UP, 1998.

Loeb, Paul Rogat, ed. *The Impossible Will Take a Little While: A Citizen's Guide to Hope in a Time of Fear*. New York: Basic Books, 2004.

——. *Soul of a Citizen: Living with Conviction in a Cynical Time*. New York: St. Martin's Griffin, 1999.

"Lutheran Volunteer Corps." 20 May 2006. <http://www.lutheranvolunteercorps.org/index.htm>.

McIntosh, Peggy. "Examining Unearned Privilege." *Liberal Education* 79.1 (1993): 61–63.

Moore, Marianne. "I May, I Might, I Must." *O to Be a Dragon*. New York: Viking, 1959. 10.

National Training Laboratories. "The Learning Pyramid." *The Texas Center for Service-Learning*. 22 May 2006. <www.txcsl.org/resources/powerpoint/STARSimp.ppt>.

Neafsey, John. *A Sacred Voice Is Calling: Personal Vocation and Social Conscience*. Maryknoll, NY: Orbis, 2006.

Pateman, Carole. *Participation and Democratic Theory*. New York: Cambridge UP, 1970.

Paul, Shale. "The Top 10 Steps for Choosing a Career." *Resource Center, Coach University*. 1996. 10 February 2006. <http://www.topten.org/content/tt.AB6.htm>.

Rattray, David. "Conflict Resolution Workshop." *First Nations, CanTeach*. 29 March 2006. <http://www.canteach.ca/elementary/fnations61.html>.

Rhoads, Robert A. *Community Service and Higher Learning: Explorations of the Caring Self*. Albany: State U of NY P, 1997.

"Social Change Wheel: Models of Community Involvement." Adapted by Career and Community Learning Center, University of Minnesota, from a publication by Minnesota Campus Compact. 1996. <http://www.csbsju.edu/csbcampusministry/03template/weel.doc>.

Takaki, Ronald. "Plenary Address: Ethical Leadership in a Multicultural World." Faith and Reason Symposium. Concordia College-Moorhead, MN. October 2003.

Taylor, Jeff. *Monster Careers: How to Land the Job of Your Life*. New York: Penguin, 2004.

Toole, James. "Levels of Engagement Chart." St. Paul: Compas Institute, 2000.

Toole, James, and Pamela Toole. "Reflection as a Tool for Turning Service Experiences into Learning Experiences." *Enriching the Curriculum through Service-Learning*. Ed. Carol W. Kinsley and Kate McPherson. Alexandria: Association for Supervision and Curriculum Development, 1995. 99–114.

U.S. Census Bureau. "Table 1a—All Races: Percent of High School and College Graduates of the Population 15 Years and Over." *Current Population Survey*. 3 January 2006. <http://www.census.gov/population/socdemo/education/cps2004/tab01a-01.xls>.

Valerius, Laura, and Michelle L. Hamilton. "The Community Classroom: Serving to Learn and Learning to Serve." *College Student Journal* 35.3 (Sept. 2001): 339. Academic Search Premier. <http://web102.epnet.com>.

Wackerle Career and Leadership Center. "Alternative Spring Break." *Monmouth College*. 25 May 2006. <http://www.monm.edu/wackerle/alternative-spring-break.htm>.

Waldstein, Fredric A. "The Value and Rationale for Combining Service and Learning: Personal Reflections." *Journey to Service-Learning: Experiences from Independent*

*Liberal Arts Colleges and Universities.* Eds. Robert L. Sigmon and Stephen G. Pelletier. Washington: Council of Independent Colleges, 1996. 70-73.

Wall, Thomas. *Thinking Critically about Philosophical Problems.* Belmont, CA: Wadsworth/Thomson Learning, 2001.

Walter, Timothy L., Glenn M. Knudsvig, and Donald E. P. Smith. *Critical Thinking: Building the Basics.* 2nd ed. Belmont, CA: Thomson Wadsworth, 2003.

Weigert, Kathleen. "Academic Service-Learning: Its Meaning and Relevance." *New Directions for Teaching and Learning* 73 (1998): 3-10.

Westheimer, Joel, and Joseph Kahne. "What Kind of Citizen? The Politics of Educating for Democracy." *American Educational Research Journal* 41.2 (Summer 2004): 237-269.

Yankelovich, Daniel. *Coming to Public Judgment.* Syracuse: Syracuse UP, 1991.

# Index

abstract conceptualization, 17, 18–19, 20
abstract thinking, 73–74
academic rigor, 11–14
academic skills, 71–75
acceptance, 56
action
    in CARC Learning Cycle, 106, 112–114
    defined, 112
    intellectual skills, 113, 114
    physical labor, 113, 114
    recording, 114
    social and emotional support, 113, 114
active experimentation, 17, 19, 20
active listening, 58
active orientation, of teams, 60
Adopt-a-Grandparent, 76, 113
ally, 67
Alma College, Michigan, 32
alternative break programs, 32–33
American Colleges and Universities (AACU),
    39, 69, 70
AmeriCorps, 34–35, 47
AmeriCorps*NCCC (National Civilian
    Community Corps), 34–35
AmeriCorps*VISTA (Volunteers in Service to
    America), 34
anticipation, 108
applied contemplation, 44
ARC, 113
Aristotle, 43–48, 94, 108
"Assessing Community Service-Learning: Are
    We Identifying the Right Outcomes?"
    (Kezar), 96
assessment, 95–101
    instruments, 100
    learning outcomes, 96–101
    objectives, 95
    portfolios, 99
    value reflection, 98
Asset-Based Community Development
    Institute, Northwestern
    University, 111n
asset mapping, 111–112
Association of American Colleges and
    Universities (AACU), 31
attitudinal scales, 110
authenticity, 56–57
Autry, James, 56
avoidance of conflict, 57–58

Barber, Benjamin R., 16, 41
Battistoni, Richard M., 41
Beer, Jennifer E., 26
Be Globally Focused, 75–76
behavior, 112
being present to others, 56–57
being useful, 56
Bereiter, Carl, 70n
Berkeley Career Center, 82
Bloom's Taxonomy, 110
Bono (Paul Hewson), 47
Boyle, Harry, 16
Break Away, 32
Bricker-Jenkins, Mary, 80
Bringle, Robert J., 117
Buechner, Frederick, 80–81
*Building Communities from the Inside Out*
    (Kretzmann and McKnight), 111n

calling, 80–83. *See also* careers; employment
Campus Compact, 21, 31
campus facilitators, 11, 92–93
campus organizations, 93
campus-wide initiatives, 30–31
CARC Learning Cycle, 17, 105–125
    action, 106, 112–114
    commitment, 106, 122–125
    contemplation, 106–112
    reflection, 106, 115–121
Career Center, Berkeley, 82
careers. *See also* employment; vocation
    preparing for, 84–87
    vocations, 80–83
carpooling, 102
celebrities, 47
Centenary College, Louisiana, 33
Center for Social Justice Research, Teaching
    and Service, Georgetown University, 69
challenging reflection, 117, 119
Chamberlain, Craig, 79
Chowdhury, Anwarul K., 52
*Chronicle of Higher Education, The,*
    21–22, 84
citizenship, 39–67
    Aristotelian philosophy and, 43–48
    education as preparation for, 39
    engaged, 48–55
    ethnic diversity and, 62
    good life, 43–44

citizenship (*cont.*)
  as one of Seven C's, 56–57
  participatory citizens, 48–51
  personally responsible citizens, 48–51
  qualities of, 45–46
  stereotypes and, 63–64
  transforming citizens, 48–55
  value of, 43–46
civic engagement, 30
civic responsibility, 16–17, 115
civility, controversy with, 56, 57
class, 62–63
  stereotypes, 63
classical Greek philosophy, 43–48
clients, 93–94
CoachVille, 82
cognitive skills, 71–75. *See also* thinking
Colby, Ann, 67
collaboration, 56, 78, 80
college
  rules and regulations of, 112
  selecting, 85–86
  as separate realm, 91
commitment
  in CARC Learning Cycle, 106, 122–125
  defined, 122
  as one of Seven C's, 56
  projection exercise, 123–124
  to service, 123–125
  to volunteering, 122
commonality, 7–8
common purpose, 56, 57
communication
  breakdown in, 52
  community discussions, 102
  confidentiality, 27
  cultural differences and, 25–28
  employment and, 86
  listening, 27, 53–54
  open style, 76
  organizing, 101–102
  personal manifesto, 52–55
  precise, 73, 75
  social and interpersonal skills, 75–80
  speech, 54–55
  style, 27
  words, 52–53
communication context, 26–28
"Communication Tools for Understanding
  Cultural Differences" (LeBaron), 26
Communities Organized for Public Service
  (COPS), 48
community
  being an ally to, 67
  connectedness to, 9
  defined, 7

  healthy, 45
  identifying, 7–9
  individuality and, 39–40, 43
  personal, 7–9
  service-learning and, 46–47
  Social Change Wheel, 66, 67
community-based learning, 4, 7
community body (polity), 41
community discussions, 102
Community Model for Conflict
  Resolution, 57–58
community partners
  action stage, 112–114
  as coeducators, 13
  commitment to, 7–11
  communicating with, 27
  contemplation with, 111–112
  course-embedded service-learning and, 22
  evaluation role, 14
  on-site orientation, 113–114
  relationships with, 28
  role of, 9, 11, 93–94
  selecting, 23, 114
community service, 4
  defined, 5
  by ordinary citizens, 47–48
*Community Service and Higher Learning*
  (Rhoads), 43
compassionate connectedness, 80
competence, 77
compromise, 57–58
Computer Support Services, 58–59
Concordia College, Moorhead, MN, 30
concrete experience, 17–18, 19–20
Cone, Richard, 41
confidence, 77–78
confidentiality, 27, 112
conflict resolution
  avoidance, 57–58
  community model for, 57–58
  confrontation, 57–58
  problem-solving, 58–59
confrontation, 57–58
congruence, 56, 57
connected reflection, 117, 118–119
consciousness of self, 56, 57
contemplation
  anticipation in, 108
  in CARC Learning Cycle, 106–112
  with community partner, 111–112
  defined, 112
  group, 109–111
  individual, 108–109
contextualized reflection, 117, 119
continuous reflection, 117–118
controversy with civility, 56, 57

cooperative education, 4, 5
Coplin, Bill, 84, 85
Cornwell, Grant H., 31-32
Corporation for National and Community
    Service, 34
corporations, 40-41
course-embedded service-learning, 22-29
    direct services, 24-28
    evaluation methods, 13-14
    group, 23-24
    indirect services, 28-29
    individual, 23-24
    long-term, 24
    optional, 22-23
    participation points, 22
    required, 22-23
    short term, 24
courtesy, 112
court-ordered volunteer work, 5
creative arts, reflection through, 121
creative thinking, 73, 74-75
critical comprehension, 71
critical inquiry, 40
critical thinking, 115
    components of, 73-75
    skills, 13, 73
    skills development, 74
*Critical Thinking: Building the Basics*
    (Walter, Knudsvig, and Smith), 73
cultural differences, 25-28
Cureton, Jeannette S., 78

data collection, 29
decision-making skills, 86
democracy
    civic responsibility, 16-17
    individual participation in, 46
    service-learning and, 41-43
    values, 43-46
*Democracy and Education*
    (Dewey), 106
demonstrations, 12
Dewey, John, 17, 105-106, 115, 116, 117
Dillon, Peter, 96
direct course-embedded
    service-learning, 24-28
diversity, 60-67
    class, 62-63
    gender, 62-63, 63
    privilege, 64-67
    race, 61-62
    stereotypes, 63-64
domestic politics, 31
doubt, 116-117
dress, 112
Duncan, Dawn, 51-55, 56

Eastern Michigan University, 30
economy, 70
*Educating Citizens: Preparing America's
    Undergraduates for Lives of Moral and
    Civic Responsibility* (Colby), 67
education. *See also* learning
    academic and cognitive skills and, 71-75
    economic competitiveness and, 70
    as preparation for citizenship, 39
    reorganization of, 70
    service-learning benefits, 69-71
    transferable intellectual capacity, 69
*Education for Democracy* (Barber and
    Battistoni), 41
efficacy, 77
Ellingboe, Brenda J., 76
emotional support, 113, 114
employment. *See also* vocation
    preparing for, 84-87
    service-learning and, 33-34
    skills for, 84-87
    worklife unreadiness, 84-85
engaged citizenship, 48-55
    levels of, 48-51
    personal case, 51-55
    service site selection and, 114
    tracing levels of, 51
environmental impact policy, 42
Equipped for the Future (EFF) Standards,
    86-87
ethical leadership, 40-41
ethics, 28
ethnicity, 60, 61-62
evaluation methods, 13-14
Evaluation System for Experiential Education
    (ESEE), 99
experience, skills gained, 84, 85
experiential learning, 17-20, 105-106
*Experiential Learning* (Dewey), 106
experiential learning directors, 92
Eyler, Janet, 42, 75, 77, 108, 117, 118,
    119, 122

facilitators
    identification of learning outcomes by, 11
    service-learning roles, 92-93, 115
faculty, 92, 109-110, 115
faith-based initiatives, 35
Figler, Howard E., 47
Five Ways of Being, 56-57
forked-road situations, 116-117
foundational skills, 69
frustration, 116-117
fundraising, 29
Furco, Andrew, 99
Fusion, 30

Gardner, John N., 73–75
gender, 63
gender roles, 63
generosity, 45
Giles, Dwight E., 42, 75, 77, 117, 118, 119, 122
global economy, 70
global learning, 31–32
good life, 43–44, 48
grading, 98–99
graduation requirements, 33–34
grant writing, 29
Gray, Charlene J., 75
*Greater Expectations: A New Vision for Learning as a Nation Goes to College* (AACU), 39–67, 69, 70
Greek philosophy, 43–48
Greenleaf Center for Servant-Leadership, 55–56
group contemplation, 109–111
group course-embedded service-learning, 23–24

Habitat for Humanity, 32, 113
Halford, Joan Montgomery, 62, 63
Hall, Edward T., 25–26
Hands for Change, 30, 109–110
happiness, 45
Hatcher, Julie A., 117
Hewson, Paul (Bono), 47
high-context communication, 26–28
Hollander, Elizabeth, 21
*How We Think* (Dewey), 116, 117
human purpose, 44

incidental learners, 70
indirect course-embedded service-learning, 28–29
individual contributions, 28
individual course-embedded service-learning, 23–24
individuality, 39–40, 43
institutional barriers, 63
integrative thinkers, 70–71
intellectual skills
    class and, 63
    service-learning action, 113, 114
    value of, 69
intentional learners, 70–71
intentional reciprocal partnerships, 4
intentional reflective thinking, 14–15, 115
intercultural communication, 25–28
internships, 4, 5
interpersonal skills, 75–80
    employment and, 86
Iowa State University, 30
Irwin, Terence, 43, 44

Japanese and Exchange Teaching (JET), 35
Jewler, A. Jerome, 73–75
Jolie, Angelina, 47
justice, 45
Justice Journey, 31, 73, 75

Kahne, Joseph, 48n
Kearns, David T., 70
Kezar, Adrianna, 96, 99
Kivel, Paul, 67
Kivisto, Peter, 60, 63, 64n
Know-How Score, 84, 85
Knudsvig, Glenn M., 73
Kolb, David A., 17–20
Kolb experiential learning cycle, 17–20
Kretzmann, John P., 111n

LaNave, Kevin, 98
Larson, Carl, 59, 60
leadership, 55–60
    effective, 57
    ethical, 40–41
    ethical behavior, 40
    servant-leadership, 55–56
    skills, 30
learning, 11–14. *See also* education
    active, 97
    emancipation through, 43
    experiential, 105–106
    incidental, 70
    intentional, 70
    lifelong, 86
    retention rate, 12
Learning in Community (LINC), 78
learning objectives, 5, 94–101
    brainstorming, 110
    identifying, 11
    matching to service-learning activities, 101
learning outcomes, 94–101
    assessment, 99–100
    examples, 99
    identifying, 11, 96
Learning Patch, 6
Learning Pyramid, 11–13
LeBaron, Michelle, 26
lectures, 12
LeFasto, Frank, 59, 60
Letter to Myself, 108–109
Levinas, Emmanuel, 41
Levine, Arthur, 78
Levine, Mel, 84–85
Lewin, Kurt, 17
lifelong learning, 86
listening
    academic and cognitive skills and, 72–73
    active, 58

conflict resolution and, 58
learning, 53-54
reflection through, 120-121
tips for, 27
value of, 53
Litchfield, Bruce, 78
local politics, 31
Loeb, Paul Rogat, 46, 47, 48
long term course-embedded
    service-learning, 24
low-context communication, 26-28
Lutheran Volunteer Corps, 35

McIntosh, Peggy, 64
McKnight, John L., 111n
meaningful experiences, 29
mentors, 30, 109-110
Minnesota Campus Compact, 67
Monmouth College, 33
Moore, Marianne, 125
morals, 40
multiculturalism, 63
multimedia, 121

National Institute for Literacy, 86
National S.E.E.D. Project on Inclusive
    Curriculum, 64
National Training Laboratories, 11
Neafsey, John, 81
New Americans program, 43
Nichomachean Ethics (Aristotle), 108
Nicomachus, 94
North Carolina Central University, 33
notebooks, 97, 102, 103

one-to-one relationships, 25
openness
    in communication, 76
    team success and, 59
organization
    communication, 101-102
    for service-learning, 101-104
orientation week, 30, 109-110
outcomes assessment, 99-100

participation points, 22
participatory citizens, 48-51
    characteristics, 49
    defined, 50
    personal case, 51
participatory democracy, 43, 46
Pateman, Carole, 43
Paul, Shale, 82-83
performing arts, 121
personal fulfillment, 81
personally responsible citizens, 48-51

characteristics, 49
defined, 50
personal case, 51
personal manifestos
    communication, 52-55
    creating, 56
personal style, 60
Personal Vocation and Social Conscience, 81
Pew Charitable Trusts, 31
physical labor, 113, 114
Piaget, Jean, 17
political issues
    civic responsibility and, 16
    public judgment about, 41
    study abroad and, 31-32
polity, 41
portfolios, 99
Portland State University, 33
practical experience, 84, 85
precise communication, 73, 75
prejudice, 63
preparedness, 103
presentation skills, 72-73
present to others, being, 56, 57
privilege, 64-67
    recognizing, 64, 65, 67
    unearned, 65
problem-solving
    for conflict resolution, 58-59
    teams and, 59-60
projection exercise, 123
Project Open Hand, 32
public judgment, 41

race, 61-62
Raise Your Voice Campaign, 31
Ramirez, Virginia, 47-48, 50
reading, learning through, 12
receiving, 45
reflection
    in CARC Learning Cycle, 106, 115-121
    challenging, 117, 119
    connected, 117, 118-119
    contextualized, 117, 119
    continuous, 117-118
    defined, 14
    effective, 15
    four C's of, 117
    guidelines, 118
    intentional learning and, 71
    practicing from multiple perspectives, 15
    strategies, 120-21
    value of, 14-15, 115, 116, 119-120
reflection journals, 29
reflective observation, 17, 18, 20
respect, 112

retention rate, 12
Rhodes, Robert, 43, 46

Salt Lake Community College, 32
Scardamalia, Marlene, 70n
schedules, 102, 103
Schmiede, Angela, 117–119
Scribes and Scrolls, 113
self-awareness, 79
self-confidence, 77
self-consciousness, 56, 57
*Servant Leader, The: How to Build a Creative Team, Develop Great Morale, and Improve Bottom-Line Performance* (Autry), 56
servant-leadership, 55–56
service agencies, 93
service-learning. *See also* course-embedded service-learning
 academic and cognitive skills and, 71–75
 alternative break programs, 32–33
 assessment, 95–101
 benefits of, 6, 42–43, 45, 48–55, 67, 122–125
 campus-wide initiatives, 30–31
 challenges in, 25–29
 college selection and, 85–86
 communication challenges, 25–28
 community and, 46–47
 connecting college and everyday world with, 91–92
 course-embedded, 22–29
 defined, 4
 democracy and, 41–43
 educational benefits of, 69–71
 end-of-course displays, 123–124
 evaluation methods, 13–14
 examples, 112, 113
 expectations for, 101
 future employment and, 33–34
 goals, 95
 graduation requirements, 33–34
 intentional learning and, 71
 organization for, 101–104
 practicing, 21–35
 scheduling, 102, 103
 social confidence and, 77–78
 specifying, 30
 study abroad, 31–32
 teams and, 60
 training for, 113–114
 traits of, 7
 types of, 5
 vocation and, 82–83
Service-Learning Cycle, 106

service-learning directors, 92
service-learning movement, 21–22
service-learning notebooks, 97, 102, 103
service-learning sites
 behavior for, 112
 career skills and, 84
 dress for, 112
 learning about, 10
 orientation by, 113–114
 student selection of, 23, 114
Seven C's, 56–57
sex, 63
short term course-embedded service-learning, 24
site supervisors
 communication with, 101–102
 folders for, 103
 responsibilities of, 93
Smith, Donald E. P., 73
social barriers
 awareness of, 64
 breaking down, 62
 recognizing, 60–61
 stereotypes, 63
Social Change Wheel, 66, 67
social class, 62–63
social confidence, 77–78
social inequities, 67
social skills, 75–80
social support, 113, 114
soul, activity of, 44, 45
*Soul of a Citizen: Living with Conviction in a Cynical Time* (Loeb), 46–48
speaking
 academic and cognitive skills and, 72–73
 reflection through, 120–121
 responsibility in, 54–55
Stark, Donna, 6
stereotypes
 awareness of, 64
 class, 63
 overcoming, 63–64
 racial and ethnic, 61–62
Stoddard, Eve W., 31–32
student affairs personnel, 92–93
student participants
 coordinating with, 101–102
 roles of, 94
study abroad, 31–32
supportiveness, teams and, 60
systemic barriers, 63
systemic thinking, 73, 75

Takaki, Ronald, 61–63
Teach for America, 35
teaching methods, 12

teams and teamwork, 59-60
   challenges of, 78-79
   effective traits, 59-60
   problem-solving and, 59-60
   service-learning and, 60
   skills for, 78-79
teamwork factors, 59
technology, 121
*10 Things Employers Want You to Learn in College* (Coplin), 84
thinking
   abstract, 73-74
   creative, 73, 74-75
   critical, 13, 73-75, 115
   intentional reflective, 14-15, 115
   reflective, 14-15
   systemic, 73, 75
Toole, James, 46, 48*n*, 69, 106
Toole, Pam, 46, 69, 106
training, 113
transferable skills, 69
transforming citizens, 48-55
   characteristics, 49
   defined, 50-51
   personal case, 51-55
tutoring programs, 116-117

Urban Plunge, 31
useful, being, 56

value reflection, 98
Van Riper, Robyn, 96
virtuous character, 45
vocation. *See also* careers; employment
   exploring, 80-83

personal fulfillment and, 80-81
   preparing for, 84-87
volunteering, 4, 5
   commitment to, 122
   service-learning roles, 93
   student experience, 22
"Voting and Beyond: Engaging Students in Our Representative Democracy" (Cone), 41
vulnerability, 56, 57

Waldstein, Fredric A., 39-40, 43
Walter, Timothy L., 73
Watson, Lilla, 80
Weigert, Kathleen, 69
Welcome Week, 30
Westheimer, Joel, 48*n*
*When Hope and Fear Collide: A Portrait of Today's College Students* (Levine and Cureton), 78
*When Teams Work Best: 6,000 Team Members and Leaders Tell What It Takes to Succeed* (LeFasto and Larson), 59
*Where's the Learning in Service-Learning?* (Eyler and Giles), 42, 77, 122
Wiseman, Rosalind, 20
words, power of, 52-53
"Words Made Manifest" (Duncan), 52-55
working knowledge factors, 59
worklife unreadiness, 84-85
writing, reflection through, 120

YWCA Empowerment for Girls, 19-20, 97, 113, 115-116